Small Firms as Innovators
From Innovation to Sustainable Growth

Series on Technology Management*

Series Editor: J. Tidd (University of Sussex, UK)   ISSN 0219-9823

Published

*The complete list of the published volumes in the series can be found at
http://www.worldscientific.com/series/stm

SERIES ON TECHNOLOGY MANAGEMENT – VOL. 25

Small Firms as Innovators
From Innovation to Sustainable Growth

Helena Forsman

University of Tampere, Finland

ICP

Imperial College Press

Published by

Imperial College Press
57 Shelton Street
Covent Garden
London WC2H 9HE

Distributed by

World Scientific Publishing Co. Pte. Ltd.
5 Toh Tuck Link, Singapore 596224
USA office: 27 Warren Street, Suite 401-402, Hackensack, NJ 07601
UK office: 57 Shelton Street, Covent Garden, London WC2H 9HE

Library of Congress Cataloging-in-Publication Data
Forsman, Helena.
  Small firms as innovators : from innovation to sustainable growth / by Helena Forsman.
    pages cm. -- (Series on technology management, ISSN 0219-9823 ; vol. 25)
  Includes bibliographical references and index.
  ISBN 978-1-78326-633-3
  1. Small business--Growth. 2. Diffusion of innovations. 3. Technological innovations. I. Title.
  HD62.7.F66 2015
  338.6'42--dc23
                                    2014049698

British Library Cataloguing-in-Publication Data
A catalogue record for this book is available from the British Library.

In-house Editors: Alisha Nguyen/Dipasri Sardar

Typeset by Stallion Press
Email: enquiries@stallionpress.com

Printed in Singapore

Contents

Acknowledgments

I have had an opportunity to interact with hundreds of small business owner-managers over the last decade. This book is in large part the result of that interaction. Through a series of research projects, executive education programs and conversations, I have learned much about what it takes to successfully innovate, compete and grow. I owe my deep gratitude to all those owner-managers from whom I have learned so much.

I have benefited greatly from a wide variety of research that has preceded this publication. However, the research project "*Growth Processes in Small Firms*" inspired me to write this book. I gratefully acknowledge the financial support provided for this project by the Association of Private Entrepreneurs and the Otto Malm Foundation. There are a number of colleagues and research partners who have offered constructive feedback on the manuscript. It was immensely helpful, and I am much indebted to all of them. Particular acknowledgment needs to be made to my good friend and colleague Pirkko Airas who has provided detailed comments and suggestions for finalizing the text.

I want to sincerely thank my fantastic family for their patience and unswerving support for my work on this book even when it meant changing holiday plans and schedules or pushing the family responsibilities into second place. Finally, I owe my warmest thanks to Markku, Jarkko and Lauri for critical reading and helpful suggestions.

About the Author

 Dr. Helena FORSMAN has served the University of Tampere (Finland) in the capacity of a Professor in Business Management and the University of Winchester (UK) as a Reader in Innovation and Entrepreneurship. In addition, she is providing leadership in the fields of knowledge exchange and entrepreneurship. Helena has more than 15 years' management experience in practical-oriented RD projects aiming at fostering business development and innovation, such as the ramp up of business and knowledge centers, RD departments and business incubation activities.

Helena's research interest focuses on business development and innovation management in the context of small business. She is especially interested in how the changes in competitive landscape are forcing small firms to change the way they innovate and run their businesses. She has been a productive author of academic publications. Recently, her articles have been published in *Regional Studies*, *International Journal of Innovation Management*, *Business Strategy and the Environment*, *European Journal of Innovation Management*, *International Journal of Technology Management and Research Policy*.

Chapter 1

Introduction

The vast majority of all firms are small in size. However, there is nothing small in their influence on the regional and national economies. These firms create substantial value to the economy in terms of employment, job creation and value added. For that reason, the abilities of these firms to innovate are extremely important not only for strengthening their competitiveness but also because they through the linkages and knowledge spillovers with other firms influence the entire economy [European Commission, 2012a]. This book focuses on the small business sector. It contributes to current discussion by exploring how small firms innovate, compete and grow.

Typically small firms comprise above 95% of private sector firms [Lejárraga et al., 2014]. For example, in the European Union, the share of small firms is almost 99% which equates to 40% of value added [European Commission, 2013]. However, the lion's share of all firms are micro businesses with fewer than 10 employees. The reports published by the OECD [2013] and the World Bank [2012] show similar patterns on all continents. The small business sector has become a backbone of all economies [Lejárraga et al., 2014]. The more the development of an economy is based on growth in the service sectors, the more it accommodates small firms [Koster and Rai, 2008]. Small firms dominate service businesses especially within the wholesale and retail, professional, scientific and technical services, accommodation and food, administrative and support services, real estate activities as well as information and communication sectors. As regards the manufacturing businesses, the utilities sector, mining and quarrying as well as the construction sectors accommodate a large proportion of small firms. [European Commission, 2013.]

The firms smaller in size are also the biggest contributors to employment and job creation across the economies [cf. Neumark *et al.*, 2011; de Wit and de Kok, 2014]. In the European Union small businesses provide 50% of all jobs from which micro firms account for 30% and small firms approximately 20% [European Commission, 2013]. The small business sector also creates the majority of all new jobs. About 85% of new jobs are created by small and medium-sized enterprises (SMEs). Within this size class, micro businesses are the fastest growing group. They alone are responsible for 58% of total net employment growth while their share of total employment is much lower (20%) [European Commission, 2012b].

The figures are quite similar in the US and China. In the US the contribution of SMEs to employment is 50% and new job creation between 60% and 80% while in China the figures are 73% for employment and from 75% to 80% for new job creation [Lejárraga *et al.*, 2014].

In regard to employment, small firms seem to be more resilient to the economic downturn compared with their large counterparts [European Commission, 2013]. Nevertheless, simultaneous job creation and destruction characterize all economies and small firms play also a critical role in job destruction. Each year, millions of jobs are created by new or existing businesses as a result of growth. At the same time, millions of jobs are destroyed as a result of contraction or close of business [Haltiwanger, 2012]. Especially the service businesses account for a large share of job creation as well as job destruction [cf. Hijzen *et al.*, 2010]. Another dynamic group consists of young firms. They tend to yield a rapid growth rate balanced against a very high failure rate [Coad and Hölzl, 2009].

Innovation is considered as one of the major accelerators of employment dynamics, particularly in the creation and destruction of jobs. Innovative activities have two effects. While they can destroy jobs, they also create new ones. The product innovations stimulate employment growth through increased sales [Geroski and Machin, 1992] while the employment effects of process innovations are related to productivity changes reducing the number of employees. On the other hand, the increased productivity will result in cost reductions, and if passed to prices it may increase demand and employment [Garcia *et al.*, 2004].

Hence, innovation is closely associated with the dynamics of firm growth. However, the main goal of innovation is to transform an idea into a commercial end in a way that it will be superior in competition and generate growth and profits for the innovating firm [Forsman *et al.*, 2013]. Despite the shared understanding of the importance of innovation on growth, there is still a lack of consensus on how innovation is related to growth, especially in the small business sector. Some studies have demonstrated positive relationship, some negative, and yet others have indicated no relationship between innovation and growth [Geroski and Machin, 1992; Roper, 1997; Freel, 2000; Rochina-Barrachina *et al.*, 2010; Forsman and Temel, 2011]. On the other hand, some scholars suggest that innovation is associated to the existing performance of a firm. Hence, realized growth may drive innovation [Mason *et al.*, 2009]. This could also reflect that through their past experiences, the learning-oriented small firms have learned to grow through innovation [cf. Macpherson, 2005]. Furthermore, innovation can merely transform declining sales from the old products to growing sales from the new ones [OECD, 2010]. Thus, innovation does not necessarily generate growth but helps a firm to remain stable.

In prior studies innovation has been commonly explored as a development activity. More recently, the scholars and practitioners have suggested that innovation should rather be studied as a commercial phenomenon [cf. Freel, 2005]. This approach highlights the fact that small firms should be able to balance their exploration and exploitation capabilities. In addition to the abilities to search innovative ideas and develop innovations, small firms should also possess abilities to efficiently exploit these innovations [Forsman *et al.*, 2013]. This brings in a need to increase our understanding how small firms create their capacity to innovate as well as how these firms create their abilities to transform innovations into successful commercial ends. However, it is also essential to understand why so many firms fail in their innovative endeavors.

Hence, it can be concluded that although innovation can help small firms to grow, it also can lead to decline. However, it is important to recognize that some churning of firms and jobs belongs to a healthy economy. It can contribute substantially to productivity growth by moving resources away from less productive to more productive firms. For example, Hijzen *et al.* [2010] identified that the new entry firms are more productive than their average incumbents. Thus, the dynamism, even turbulence in the economy has a favorable impact on economic well being. [Haltiwanger, 2012.] While the majority of academic studies have been interested in job creation and the growing firms, this book explores also job destruction and the declining firms.

It is a well-documented empirical fact that small firms are essential to the healthy economy and therefore they deserve the attention of scholars, practitioners and policy-makers around the world. However, despite a growing appreciation of the importance of these firms to the regional and national economies, their influence on policy-making has been lower than their economic impact. Commonly, the larger firms are used to reflect the interests of the region while the smaller firms have been marginal players in the policy arena and thus, their needs remain unknown [Cooke *et al.*, 2005; Christopherson and Clark, 2007; Nichter and Goldmark, 2009]. On the other hand, Mason and Brown [2013] criticize that policy-making focuses too much on the early-stage technology-based young firms reflecting the fact that policy-makers view the high-technology sectors as the main source of growing firms. They continue that growth businesses comprise a heterogeneous group of firms in terms of sector, age, size and ownership, and this heterogeneity creates major challenges for policy-making.

The fact that the smallest firms are often excluded from the national examinations, leads to a situation that policy-making will not get input about the needs of smaller firms. For example, the Community Innovation Survey [CIS, 2010] that is closely linked to the policy activities of the European Union member states excludes the firms with fewer than 10 employees, that is 92.2% of all firms, from the examination [Eurostat, 2013]. Also the Oslo Manual [OECD, 2005], which is widely used in the OECD countries as a survey methodology, recommends that the target population of surveys should include the firms with at least 10 employees. On the other hand, although the harmonized surveys used to collect information are appropriate for large firms, they are only seldom appropriate for small firms characterized by unstructured processes and systems that do not fit with the concepts commonly used in surveys [Charles *et al.*,

2000; Salazar and Holbrook, 2004]. This book makes an exception. It uses data that has been collected by the tools developed for small firms. The data includes both small firms having from 10 to 49 employees as well as micro firms having from 1 to 9 employees.

Despite the significant importance of small firms to the economies, much remains to be learned about the processes and dynamics of how small firms innovate, compete and grow. This book aims at contributing to this gap by exploring how competitiveness and growth have been achieved through innovations in smaller firms. It takes readers on a journey across the spectrum of small firms as innovators drawing its evidence from both theoretical and empirical perspectives. While the empirical data used in this book has been collected from one country, Finland, there is no reason to believe that these firms differ significantly from the firms located in the other developed countries. In addition, the findings are compared with the literature that represents a variety of developed and developing countries. However, the aim of this book is not to demonstrate statistically significant relationships and causal connections. Instead, along with the journey, it provides the reader with the descriptive details that help follow the chain for reasoning behind the main story. The empirical evidence used in this book is introduced in Appendix A.1 and Table A1.1.

The key question is how to strengthen innovation and competitiveness in small firms helping them grow and prosper. The common approach to answering this question is to start from innovations and thereafter monitor how the innovations are associated with the performance and growth of a firm. This approach has led to the interpretations suggesting that there is only one single pathway from innovations towards success. This book takes another approach. In order to reveal the possible alternative pathways, it starts by exploring what kinds of innovators the small firms are. Based on it, the four innovation performer profiles are identified for small firms. Thereafter, the characteristics of the innovator profiles are illustrated. The journey continues by examining the innovation capacity of these profiles and how competitiveness is created and maintained by them. This is followed by an exploration how competitiveness is turned into growth along with the period of 10 years. On the contrary, it also examines how small firms have lost their competitiveness resulting in declining progress. Finally, a conceptual framework for the innovation engine in small firms is presented.

This book focuses on small and micro firms. By definition, small firms encompass all firms with fewer than 50 employees and annual sales less than 10 million euros while micro firms are very small firms with fewer than 10 employees and their annual sales are below 2 million euros. Also medium-sized firms emerge from the literature. This size category comprises the firms having fewer than 250 employees and their annual sales are less than 50 million euros. [European Commission, 2003.]

The journey for exploring *Small Firms as Innovators* will be offered as follows:

Chapter 2 — Innovation Patterns in Small Firms

This chapter provides a comprehensive picture of innovation patterns in small firms. It starts by presenting the typical innovation activities in small firms and the innovative outcomes created by them. Thereafter, the chapter explores how the innovation activities diversify in small firms. Based on the diversity of these activities, four innovation performer profiles are identified. This will be followed by monitoring how a firm shifts from a low innovation performer towards a high performer. Finally, the firm-related and business environment-related characteristics of four innovation performer profiles are presented.

Chapter 3 — The Capacity of Small Firms to Innovate

This chapter explores the composition of innovation capacity in small firms. It identifies first what is the level of internal resources allocated to innovation activities. However, the resources are not enough alone. Also capabilities are required to integrate, build, and reconfigure these resources. For that reason, the status of current capabilities and future goals for capability creation are illustrated by the innovation performer profiles. Nevertheless, as has been commonly argued, innovation is not anymore the domain of an individual firm. Especially small firms should collaborate for enhancing their capacity to innovate. For that reason, the benefits gained for innovation through external collaboration are explored. Finally, the question of how the innovation capacity requirements change along with the journey from the low innovation performer towards the high performer is illustrated.

Chapter 4 — From Innovations to Growth

This chapter focuses on the question of how the different kinds of innovation performers are growing. It aims to provide the reader with a multidimensional view of growth process including the periods of continuous and temporary changes. The chapter starts by discussing the relationship between innovation and growth, and the circumstances when innovation is considered as a source of growth. This will be followed by answering the question of how growth should be measured in small firms. Finally, the growth patterns of four innovation performer profiles are identified by using a combination of measures comprising market-related, efficiency-related and employment-related indicators.

Chapter 5 — Towards Superior or Lost Competitiveness

While the question of how the different kinds of innovators have achieved growth or decline is discussed in Chapter 4, in this chapter the relationship between innovation and growth are approached from another angle by focusing on the question of how small firms have achieved long-term competitive performance through innovations. The chapter starts by discussing on competitiveness and its elements in the context of small business. Based on them, a model for assessing competitiveness in small firms is designed. Thereafter, the different kinds of growers and their opposite counterparts, decliners, are identified. Finally, the competitiveness of these grower-decliner pairs are analyzed and compared by using the model designed in this chapter.

Chapter 6 — Innovation Engine to Foster Learning in Small Firms

The unique contribution of this chapter is to provide a framework of the innovation engine to small firms for learning to compete and grow. It summarizes how small firms can through the innovation activities foster their learning and chances for business success. The chapter starts by discussing how to measure innovation performance in small firms. This will be followed by the identification of the main elements and indicators for measuring innovation. Based on the above, the elements of an optimal innovation engine are illustrated for small businesses. Hence, the aim is to offer both theoretical and empirical insights for answering the questions of how to improve innovation performance in small firms, what performance dimensions should be measured or assessed in these firms and what are the appropriate indicators for doing it. Finally, this chapter provides views on how a small firm can develop its own innovation engine and how this tool can be used in decision-making for accelerating innovation.

Chapter 7 — Conclusions for Moving Forward

This chapter completes the journey. It summarizes the theme "*Small Firms as Innovators*" together with the insights that emerge out of empirical and theoretical evidence. This will be done by presenting the differences between the highly successful small firms and the majority of small firms. The behavior, characteristics, activities and processes of highly successful small firms are considered as potential elements of a success recipe for sustainable competitiveness and growth. Therefore, the High Performers are compared against the typical small firms. In addition, a set of the implications are provided for how to fill the gap between them. This comparison will be carried out by using the innovation engine as a framework.

Appendix — Details Behind the Figures

In order to provide the reader with a story-style reading experience and an easier way to follow the story and the pattern building along it, the detailed information on empirical evidence is separated from the main text. However, they are presented in the appendix.

References

Charles, D.R., Nauwelaers, C., Mouton, B. and Bradley, D. (2000). *Assessment of the Regional Innovation and Technology Transfer Strategies and Infrastructures (RITTS) Scheme.* Final Evaluation Report (CURDS and MERIT with PAIR and OIR). Online. Available at: http://cordis.europa.eu/home_en.html (Accessed 16.04.2014).

Christopherson, S. and Clark, J. (2007). Power in firm networks: What it means for regional innovation systems, *Regional Studies*, 41(9), pp. 1223–1236.

CIS (2010). *Community Innovation Survey*, 2010. (Eurostat: European Commission). Online. Available at: http://ec.europa.eu/eurostat (Accessed 14.02.2015).

Coad, A. and Hölzl, W. (2009). On the autocorrelation of growth rates, *Journal of Industry, Competition and Trade*, 9(2), pp. 139–166.

Cooke, P., Clifton, N. and Oleaga, M. (2005). Social capital, firm embeddedness and regional development, *Regional Studies*, 39(8), pp. 1065–1077.

de Wit, G. and de Kok, J. (2014). Do small businesses create more jobs? New evidence for Europe, *Small Business Economics*, 42(2), pp. 283–295.

European Commission (2003). *The new SME definition. User guide and model declaration*. Enterprise and Industry Publications. Online. Available at: http://ec.europa.eu/enterprise/policies/sme/files/sme_definition/sme_user_guide_en.pdf (Accessed 17.03.2014).

European Commission (2012a). *EU SMEs in 2012: at the Crossroads*. Annual report on Small and Medium-Sized Enterprises in the EU, 2011/12 (Rotterdam: ECORYS Nederland BV). Online. Available at: http://ec.europa.eu/enterprise/policies/sme/facts-figures-analysis/performance-review/files/supporting-documents/2012/annual-report_en.pdf (Accessed 09.04.2014).

European Commission (2012b). *Small Companies Create 85% of New Jobs*. IP/12/2016/01/2012. Press Release. Online. Available at: http://europa.eu/rapid/press-release_IP-12-20_en.htm (Accessed 10.04.2014).

European Commission (2013). *A Recovery on the Horizon? Annual Report on European SMEs*. Final Report. Online. Available at: http://ec.europa.eu/enterprise/policies/sme/facts-figures-analysis/performance-review/files/supporting-documents/2013/annual-report-smes-2013_en.pdf (Accessed 31.05.2014).

Eurostat (2013). *Structural Business Statistics*. Online. Available at: http://ec.europa.eu/eurostat/web/structural-business-statistics/overview (Accessed 14.02.2015).

Forsman, H. and Temel, S. (2011). Innovation and business performance in small enterprises. An enterprise-level analysis, *International Journal of Innovation Management*, 15(3), pp. 641–665.

Forsman, H., Temel, S. and Uotila, M. (2013). Towards sustainable competitiveness: Comparison of the successful and unsuccessful eco-innovators, *International Journal of Innovation Management*, 17(3).

Freel, M.S. (2000). Do small innovating firms outperform non-innovators? *Small Business Economics*, 14(3), pp. 195–210.

Freel, M. (2005). The characteristics of innovation-intensive small firms: Evidence from "Northern Britain", *International Journal of Innovation Management*, 9(4), pp. 401–429.

Garcia, A., Jaumandreu, J. and Rodriguez, C. (2004). *Innovation and jobs*: *Evidence from manufacturing firms.* MPRA Paper No. 1204. Online. Available at: http://mpra.ub.uni-muenchen.de/1204/1/MPRA_paper_1204.pdf (Accessed 17.03.2014).

Geroski, P. and Machin, S. (1992). Do innovating firms outperform non-innovators? *Business Strategy Review*, 3(2), pp. 79–90.

Haltiwanger, J. (2012). *Innovation Policy and the Economy*, Volume 12, eds. Lerner, J. and Stern, S. Chapter 2 "Job Creation and Firm Dynamics in the U.S." (University of Chicago Press Journals), pp. 17–38. Online. Available at: http://www.nber.org/chapters/c12451.pdf (Accessed 17.03.2014).

Hijzen, A., Upward, R. and Wright, P.W. (2010). Job creation, job destruction and the role of small firms: Firm-level evidence for the UK, *Oxford Bulleting of Economics and Statistics*, 72(5), pp. 621–647.

Koster, S. and Rai, S.K. (2008). Entrepreneurship and economic development in a developing country: A case study of India, *The Journal of Entrepreneurship*, 17(2), pp. 117–137.

Lejárraga, I., López Rizzo, H., Oberhofer, H., Stone, S. and Shepherd, B. (2014). *SMEs in Global Markets: A Differential Approach for Services* (OECD). Online. Available at: http://www.oecd-ilibrary.org (Accessed 14.02.2015).

Macpherson, A. (2005). Learning how to grow: Resolving the crisis of knowing, *Technovation*, 25(10), pp. 1129–1140.

Mason, G., Bishop, K. and Robinson, C. (2009). *Business growth and innovation*: *The wider impact of rapidly-growing firms in UK city-regions*, Research Report (NESTA). Online. Available at: http://www.nesta.org.uk/assets/documents/business_growth_and_innovation_report (Accessed 04.10.2013).

Mason, C. and Brown, R. (2013). Creating good public policy to support high-growth firms, *Small Business Economics*, 40(2), pp. 211–225.

Neumark, D., Wall, B. and Zhang, J. (2011). Do small businesses create more jobs? New evidence for the United States from the national establishment time series, *The Review of Economics and Statistics*, 93(1), pp. 16–29.

Nichter, S. and Goldmark, L. (2009). Small firm growth in developing countries, *World Development*, 37(9), pp. 1453–1464.

OECD (2005). *Oslo Manual, Guidelines for Collecting and Interpreting Innovation Data*, (A joint publication of OECD and Eurostat). Online. Available at: http://www.oecd.org/science/inno/2367580.pdf (Accessed 14.02.2015).

OECD (2010). *High-Growth Enterprises: What Governments Can Do to Make a Difference*, OECD Studies on SMEs and Entrepreneurship. (OECD Publishing).

OECD (2013). *OECD Factbook 2013. Economic, Environmental and Social Statistics*, (OECD Publishing). Online. Available at: http://www.oecd-ilibrary. org/ (Accessed 16.11.2013).

Rochina-Barrachina, M.E., Mañez, J.A. and Llopis, J.A. (2010). Process innovations and firm productivity growth, *Small Business Economics*, 34(2), pp. 147–166.

Roper, S. (1997). Product innovation and small business growth: A comparison of the strategies of German, UK and Irish companies, *Small Business Economics*, 9(6), pp. 523–537.

Salazar, M. and Holbrook, A. (2004). A debate on innovation surveys, *Science and Public Policy*, 31(4), pp. 254–266.

World Bank (2012). *World Development Report 2013: Jobs.* (World Bank, Washington, DC).

Chapter 2

Innovation Patterns in Small Firms

2.1 Introduction

It is a well-documented fact that innovation drives economic growth, and small firms play a vital role in stimulating both innovation and growth in all economies. The small size provides some common advantages for doing it, such as flexibility, high customer-orientation accompanied with an ability to respond, adapt and improve. In addition, small firms possess an ability to move quickly in implementing change.

On the other hand, the small size is also associated with some disadvantages such as poor opportunity identification practices, limited capabilities to screen market and technology trends, unsophisticated intelligence gathering systems, reactive attitudes towards innovation, lack of resources and difficulties in networking [e.g., Cohen and Klepper, 1996; Scozzi *et al.*, 2005; Forsman, 2008; Forsman and Rantanen, 2011]. Hansen and Serin [1997] add to this that in small firms innovation development is to a great extent based on the experiences and abilities of "practical men and women", and these practical individuals, who through learning by doing create their know-how, are also the key actors in innovation activities.

This chapter focuses on innovation activities in small firms. It starts by exploring what kinds of innovative outcomes these firms have created. Thereafter, the emphasis shifts from innovations to innovators aiming at identifying the different kinds of innovators among the small firms. Finally, the characteristics of these innovators are presented.

2.2 Innovation Activities in Small Firms

The answer to the question of what kinds of innovation activities are typical of the resource-scarce small firms depends very much on how innovation is defined. In the Oslo Manual [OECD, 2005], innovation is defined as the implementation of new or improved products and services, new marketing or organizational methods and workplace organization or external relations. Based on this definition, innovation can be seen as a broad concept that includes a wide range of activities resulting in changes in the products and services of firms as well as in the ways these products and services are delivered to the customers [Damanpour *et al.*, 2009]. These changes can lead to incremental improvements or radically new innovations. Hence, the above definition reveals two commonly used principles to classify innovation activities: the degree of difference and the degree of newness [Johannessen *et al.*, 2001].

The outcome-based approach has been widely used as a basis for the degree of difference. It commonly defines innovation as a new product or service produced in the existing way or a new process for producing and delivering the existing products and services [cf. Damanpour and Gopalakrishnan, 2001; Bessant *et al.*, 2005; de Jong and Marsili, 2006]. Hence, the product and service innovations aiming at creating new offerings to the existing markets or exploring new markets for the existing offerings have an external focus. Instead, the process innovations aiming at increasing the efficiency of internal processes for facilitating the production of these offerings have an internal focus.

Damanpour *et al.* [2009] have enhanced this two-folded typology further by dividing the process innovations into two types. They found that process innovations can be associated either with the technical or administrative system of a firm. The technical process innovations are new elements that change the operating system of a firm while the administrative process innovations mainly change the management system of a firm [Damanpour *et al.*, 2009].

In the context of small business, innovations are often developed integrated into the daily business activities and customer collaboration [Forsman, 2008; Hirsch-Kreinsen, 2008]. Hence, innovation can even be hidden in nature and people who are involved in the innovation activities do not necessarily consider the activity as innovation development but, for example, as a quality improvement or customer collaboration [Hansen and Serin, 1997]. Due to the fact that the distinction between the different innovation types is not always clear, the above product-process innovation typology has commonly been used for exploring innovation in small firms [see for example, de Jong and Marsili, 2006; Nieto and Santamaria, 2010; Forsman and Rantanen, 2011].

The activities for developing product and process innovations lead to two forms of outcomes. First, an innovation activity can lead to a completely new offering or a new way of producing and delivering it. Alternatively, it may lead to the improvement of an existing offering, process or practice [cf. Plehn-Dujowich, 2009]. This brings in the second commonly used principle for defining innovation i.e., the degree of newness. However, the question of how the degree of newness should be defined is not an easy question to be answered.

Maybe the most common approach has been to divide innovative outcomes into incrementally and radically new innovations. An innovation is considered to be incrementally new when it is an improvement to the existing offering or process while the radically new innovation is a completely new offering or process to serve new customers or new customer needs [Dewar and Dutton, 1986; Garcia and Calantone, 2002; Verhees *et al.*, 2010]. The common motivation for the development of incremental innovations is to make things better through the enhancement of existing capacity while the development of radical innovations is driven by the motivation to make things differently through the regeneration of existing capacity, the acquisition of new know-how and the allocation of significant resources [e.g., Ellonen *et al.*, 2009; Verhees *et al.*, 2010; Forsman and Annala, 2011].

Thus, the radical innovations can also be separated from the incremental ones based on the degree of change it causes in a firm [Damanpour, 1996]. According to Damanpour and Aravind [2012], the radical innovation produces fundamental changes in the activities of a firm and thus, it represents a substantial departure from the existing practices. Hence, the degree of newness of incremental innovations is commonly specified as new to the innovating firm while the degree of newness of radical innovations is specified as new to the customers, new to the entire sector or new even to the whole world [Johannessen *et al.*, 2001; Garcia and Calantone, 2002; Dahlin and Behrens, 2005; Damanpour *et al.*, 2009; Kasmire *et al.*, 2012].

The above approaches of newness emphasize the internal changes as well as the market changes. In order to capture both aspects, in this book, the innovative outcome that is new to the competitors of the innovator is considered to mirror a high degree of newness, and thus, it reflects the presence of the radical innovation activities in small firms [cf. Salazar and Holbrook, 2004; de Jong and Vermeulen, 2006]. Correspondingly, the innovative outcome that is new to the innovating firm itself reflects the presence of the incremental innovation activities [cf. Damanpour *et al.*, 2009; Forsman and Rantanen, 2011].

Hence, in order to answer the question presented at the beginning of this chapter: "*What kind of innovation activities are typical of the resource-scarce small firms?*", in this book the innovation activities of small firms are examined based on the degree of difference and the degree of newness resulting in six types of innovative outcomes: radical and incremental product/service innovations, radical and incremental technical process innovations and finally, radical and incremental administrative process innovations. These innovations are explored by using the empirical evidence from 392 small firms with fewer than 50 employees. Table 2.1 presents their innovation patterns grouped by the service and manufacturing businesses.

As can be noticed, the majority of small firms are innovators when innovation is defined broadly to cover both radical and incremental changes. In this sample, 93.4% of all firms have recently implemented at least one type of innovation. Most commonly it is an improved product or service. The activities for developing incremental innovations are more common than the activities for developing radical innovations. 88.0% of firms have developed at least one incremental innovation during the past four years while only 42.9% of them have developed at least one radical innovation. When comparing the manufacturing and service businesses, it can be noticed that the patterns of their innovation activities are quite

Table 2.1.   Innovation patterns by the manufacturing and service businesses ($N = 392$).

	Manufacturing businesses	Service businesses	Total
Radical innovation activities[a]			
Products/services	26.9	41.0	33.9
Technical processes	19.8	16.9	18.4
Administrative processes	16.8	17.9	17.3
Incremental innovation activities[a]			
Products/services	70.1	68.2	69.1
Technical processes	62.4	59.5	61.0
Administrative processes	60.9	60.0	60.5

Note: [a]Proportion of firms that have developed innovation type in question.

similar. Only one significant difference emerges. The service-intensive businesses have developed more often radical offerings to their customers than the manufacturing businesses.

When the same question of what kinds of innovation activities are typical of small firms will be put to prior literature, it provides conflicting answers. For example, Damanpour and Wischnevsky [2006] identified that radical innovations are typical in small firms (especially in young ones) while the incremental innovations dominate in large firms. Contrary to this, Forsman and Rantanen [2011] found an opposite pattern. According to them, incremental product innovations are the dominant innovative outcomes in small firms while the radical ones are less common. Instead, de Jong and Marsili [2006] recognized that in small firms the process innovations are more widespread than the product innovations. Finally, Avermaete *et al.* [2003] did not find any differences between the product and process innovations in these firms.

One reason for the conflicting results could be the differences in the firms included in the sample, for example in terms of age of firm, size of firm or industrial sector of firm. The fact how innovation is defined can be another reason. If innovation is defined broadly, the study leads to the divergent conclusions compared with the setting that only the radically new innovations are included into the examination. Therefore, given the inconclusive results of prior studies, innovation should be defined before one can answer the question of typical innovations.

However, the above outcome-based approach that focuses only on single innovations has been criticized for not being able to capture the nature of innovation activities in small firms. It has been suggested that in order to remain successful over longer periods of time, the firm should introduce a stream of innovations. In the best scenario, this means that innovation feeds innovation in a way that the output of one innovation activity will serve as the input to the next one [Avermaete *et al.*, 2003; Ambec and Lanoie, 2008; Horbach, 2008; Amara *et al.*, 2009; Damanpour *et al.*, 2009]. Hence, the firms must be able to implement both incremental and radical change [Tushman and O'Reilly, 1996]. Damanpour *et al.* [2009] add to this that the impact of innovation on the performance of a firm depends on the co-adoption of different innovation types instead of the adoption of a single type. Also Roberts and Amit [2003] suggest that establishing an attractive competitive position depends on the specific history of a firm's innovation activities. In order to figure out the effect of this history within small firms, the next chapter focuses on the diversity of innovation activities. It explores how the innovation activities diversify in small firms.

2.3 From a Low Performer to a High Performer

Forsman and Annala [2011], who have studied the combinations of innovations in small firms, found that if the firm has a small-scale history in its innovation activities, it mainly had developed incremental product or service innovations. Instead, when the diversity of innovation activities increases, the product/service innovations will be followed by the development of process/method innovations and operation modes. They also identified that at high diversity levels the firms are continuous innovators developing several types of innovations in regular occurrences.

Hence, in order to improve performance, small firms should have diversified innovation activities for creating several types of innovative outcomes. This demands turning our attention from innovations to innovators [cf. Garcia and Calantone, 2002; Freel, 2005; Damanpour *et al.*, 2009]. In order to explore the characteristics of different kinds of innovators in the sample used in this book, an innovation performer profile was specified to every firm [cf. Forsman and Annala, 2011]. The history of innovation activities is analyzed for the period of four years (2005 to 2008). Based on the developed radical and incremental innovations and the diversity of innovation activities, four profiles emerge from the empirical evidence: Low Performers, Incremental Performers, Radical Performers and High Performers.

Based on 15 innovation management practices among French firms, Boly *et al.* [2014] have identified a quite similar classification consisting of four groups: proactive, preactive, reactive and passive firms. When combining these two classifications based on the history of innovation management practices [cf. Boly *et al.*, 2014] and the history of innovation development activities [Forsman and Annala, 2011], the results reveal four quite different kinds of innovators among the firms smaller in size (see Figure 2.1).

The first profile, the Low Performers, comprises non-innovators and the firms that during the history of four years have reported about the activities for developing only one type of incremental innovation. About 15.6% of small firms in this data hold this profile. The Low Performers are close to what Boly *et al.* [2014] call the passive class. These firms are characterized by weak or non-existent innovation management practices. They rely on their current products and services and the ways how these are produced and delivered to the customers. Hence, it seems that the Low

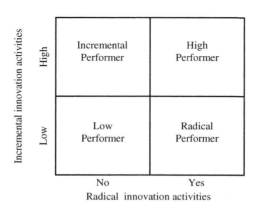

Fig. 2.1.   Innovation performer profiles.

Performers have adopted a defensive strategy for maintaining their position to survive. Change is not visible in these firms.

The second profile, the Incremental Performers, consists of firms that are entirely biased towards incremental innovation activities. These firms are occasional innovators that have reported about the activities for developing two or more incremental innovations. Thus, the diversity of innovation activities is relatively low. This group of firms is close to what Boly *et al.* [2014] have entitled as the reactive class. They are more entrepreneurial than innovative having an emphasis on adaptation to the changes in the business environment. These firms are characterized by short-term strategy, quite poor innovation management practices and low investments allocated in the RD activities. In this sample, the Incremental Performers are the largest profile, 41.6% of firms have their emphasis exclusively on implementing incremental change.

The third profile consists of firms that are biased towards radical innovation activities. Also these Radical Performers are occasional or frequent innovators with relatively low innovation diversity. In their innovation history, these firms have either no incremental innovation activities or only one minor improvement to a current product or process. This profile has similarities with the reactive class introduced by Boly *et al.* [2014]. These businesses comprise the dynamic and innovative firms that anticipate changes by adopting a medium-term vision with an emphasis on competitive technology, competence management and project management. The innovation activities are in operation but the innovation management practices are quite weak. These firms have their emphasis exclusively on implementing radical change. In this sample, 16.1% of firms hold the profile of Radical Performers.

Finally, the fourth profile, the High Performers, is characterized by the high diversity of innovation activities. These firms are continuous innovators that during the period of four years have developed three or more innovations, including both radical and incremental ones. This profile is quite similar to the proactive class introduced by Boly *et al.* [2014]. Within these firms the innovation management practices are strong for organizing the permanent procedures to facilitate the innovation activities. They have been able to implement both incremental and radical change. In this sample approximately one fourth of firms (26.8%) are the High Performers.

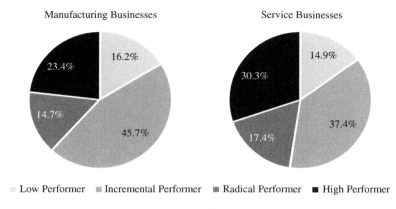

Fig. 2.2.   The distribution of four innovation performer profiles.

Figure 2.2 summarizes the distribution of four innovation performer profiles by sector while the details of innovation patterns for these profiles are presented in Appendix, Table A2.1. As can be noticed, within the manufacturing businesses the proportion of Incremental Performers is higher than within the service businesses. Correspondingly, within the service business the share of High Performers is evidently higher than within the manufacturing businesses.

The above classification demonstrates that at its best the output of one innovation becomes the input to the next innovation. This seems to be especially true among the High Performers characterized by high innovation diversity. This raises an interesting question of how a firm can shift from the position of the Low Performer to the position of the High Performer.

When tracking how innovation activities diversify in small firms, two main routes can be identified for this journey. Figure 2.3 illustrates these options.

Based on the empirical evidence used in this book, five out of six small firms have selected Route 1, in which the Low Performer starts by engaging in the incremental innovation activities for improving its current products or services. Thereafter, driven by the need to produce and deliver more efficiently these products and services, the firm improves its technical processes. Along with this progress, it moves from the position of the

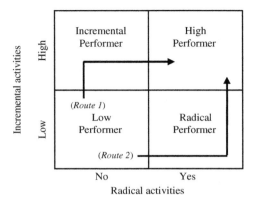

Fig. 2.3.   Two main routes towards the high performer [cf. Forsman and Temel, 2014].

Low Performer to the position of the Incremental Performer. Now, the firm is ready to expand its activities to cover also the radical innovation activities. Most commonly the firm identifies the need to change radically its administrative processes. When both the radical and incremental innovation activities have been established, the firm takes a new position as a High Performer.

Correspondingly, one out of six small firms selects Route 2 in which the firm starts by developing a radically new product or service innovation. When the radical innovation activities are established it moves from the position of the Low Performer to the position of the Radical Performer. However, it is not enough to have a new product or service, the question of how it will be produced and delivered to customers can be even more important than the radically new offering itself. Therefore, the firm on Route 2 continues by improving its technical processes. In the later stages, the firm is ready to change also its administrative processes. Route 2 ends in the same vein as Route 1. When both the radical and incremental innovation activities are established, the firm moves from the position of the Radical Performer to the position of the High Performer. Figure 2.4 exhibits the details how innovation diversifies along with the above two routes.

It can be summarized that, along with both routes, innovation feeds innovation. The developed product/service innovations imply a need to improve

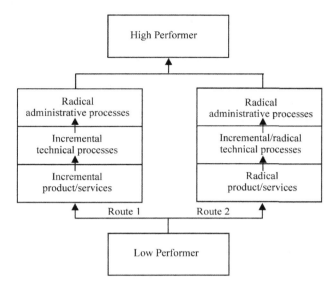

Fig. 2.4.   The details how innovation feeds innovation along with two routes.

efficiency for producing and delivering these new products and services, thus accelerating the development of technical process innovations. Further, this reveals the need for more efficient management systems, thus, stimulating the development of administrative process innovations.

Instead, there are differences in the degree of change the innovation activities create. The firms that have selected Route 1 seem to be ready to experience the radical change at the later stages of their innovation journey. In addition, they seem to have a tendency to implement radical internal change prior to commencing to implement the radical external change. Instead, the firms that have selected Route 2 first experience the radical external changes prior they commence to implement the incremental or radical internal changes.

While this section has illustrated some distinctive features of the different kinds of innovators, there is, however, a need to take a closer look at the different profiles. In order to reinforce the main characteristics of the innovation performer profiles, the next chapter focuses on the factors related to business environment.

2.4 Business Environment-Related Characteristics

When exploring innovation in small firms, one of the key questions is: 'What impact does the business environment have on innovation activities at a firm-level?' It is clear that the economic situation affects through the existence of business opportunities the abilities and willingness of firms to innovate and take risks. Between the different kinds of innovators, there are also differences in vulnerability for the unfavorable economic situation. For example, Forsman and Temel [2011] identified that the non-innovators and the innovators characterized by diversified innovation activities are among the best performing small firms during the recession. Instead, the firms with low innovation diversity may suffer during the downswing.

In addition to the availability of opportunities, business environment is related to such aspects as infrastructure [Robson and Obeng, 2008], location [Liedholm, 2002], the availability of competent staff and the functionality of innovation system [Aubert, 2005], access to finance [Galindo and Micco, 2007], the degree of corruption [Estrin *et al.*, 2013] and the regulatory environment [Ateljevic and Doorne, 2004]. A well-operating business environment provides positive incentives to innovating firms while the weaknesses of environment may impede the innovation activities. The firms smaller in size frequently report that the public policies are unpredictable. In the circumstances of uncertainty, they are not willing to allocate resources to the risky innovation activities [cf. World Bank, 2005]. Hence, the disadvantages related to the business environment give a reason to ask what the characteristics of a positive business environment are [Nichter and Goldmark, 2009].

By using the empirical evidence collected for this book, this section aims to shed light into the above question by illustrating the characteristics of the business environment in terms of four indicators: location, the satisfaction of a firm with the region and its policy-making, employee satisfaction reflecting the availability of competent staff, and finally, the use of services provided by the regional development agencies, universities and other educational institutes. Table 2.2 presents the details of the business environment-related factors.

As can be seen, there do not exist dramatic differences in location across the innovation performer profiles. The service firms are slightly

Table 2.2.   Business environment-related factors by innovation performer profiles.

	Low Performer	Incremental Performer	Radical Performer	High Performer	Total
Manufacturing businesses					
Location[a]	46.9%	44.4%	51.7%	41.3%	45.2%
Regional services[b]	6.8%	16.5%	20.7%	13.8%	14.9%
Firm satisfaction[c]	0.59	0.60	0.59	0.48	0.57
Employee satisfaction[c]	0.38	0.42	0.43	0.55	0.45
Service businesses					
Location[a]	51.7%	63.0%	64.7%	54.2%	59.0%
Regional services[b]	10.9%	18.7%	8.8%	26.8%	18.3%
Firm satisfaction[c]	0.60	0.57	0.46	0.64	0.58
Employee satisfaction[c]	0.31	0.38	0.24	0.53	0.39

Notes: [a]Proportion of firms located in the urban areas.
[b]Proportion of firms that have used the regional development services.
[c]Mean, 5-items scale with min = −2 (very unsatisfied) and max = 2 (very satisfied).

more often located in the urban areas than the manufacturing businesses. Within the service firms, the Incremental and Radical Performers are more commonly running their businesses in urban areas whereas within the manufacturing businesses, the Radical Performers are more often located in the urban areas than the other profiles.

When looking at firm satisfaction and employee satisfaction across the innovation performer profiles, it can be noticed that commonly firm satisfaction is at a higher level than employee satisfaction. In addition to this, employee satisfaction has more variation across the profiles.

Regarding the use of services provided by the regional development agencies, universities and other educational institutes (regional services), only a minority of small firms have used these services. Within the manufacturing businesses the Radical Performers have most often used the regional development and consulting services while within the service businesses, the High Performers have been the most frequent users of these services. Correspondingly, the Low Performers of the manufacturing businesses and the Radical Performers of the service businesses are infrequently seen as customers at the desks of regional services.

Hence, it seems that the High Performers of the service businesses are the most satisfied with their business environment. In addition, these firms are the most regular users of the services provided by the regional development agencies, universities and other educational institutes. Correspondingly, the Radical Performers of the service businesses are less satisfied with their business environment and they are the uncommon customers of regional development services.

One explanation for this could be the fact that the regional development services in Finland are commonly designed based on the needs and practices of technology-intensive firms. The Radical Performers within the service businesses may have experienced these services as less appropriate for them. On the other hand, the High Performers are very satisfied. This leads to suggest that there might be differences in the capabilities that explain this somewhat conflicting finding. The High Performers with their sophisticated innovation management practices may have better abilities to exploit the regional services than the Radical Performers with their quite weak innovation management practices. However, the low usage of regional development services gives a reason to ask whether there is a cognitive gap between small firms and regional service providers.

Nevertheless, the firm-related factors may also affect the abilities of firms to exploit the opportunities their business environment offers. Hence, the next chapter focuses on the firm-related characteristics of innovation performer profiles.

2.5 Firm-Related Characteristics

The firm-related factors such as size and age have commonly been connected with the innovation activities of firms. In addition, the rise of the service economy has stimulated a discussion whether there are differences between the manufacturing-intensive and service-intensive sectors. However, several studies have shown that the industrial sectors are not internally homogeneous [e.g., Amable and Palombarini, 1998; de Jong and Marsili, 2006; Kirner *et al.*, 2009; Forsman, 2011]. For example, Evangelista [2000] found that the service and manufacturing businesses show more similarities than differences in their innovation activities. Forsman [2011] however, points out that while there are no tremendous differences between the manufacturing and service businesses, within them there are several heterogeneous groups of firms having differences

Table 2.3. Knowledge-technology intensity by the innovation performer profile.

	Low Performer	Incremental Performer	Radical Performer	High Performer	Total
Manufacturing businesses					
Know-technology intensity	%	%	%	%	%
Supplier-dominated	62.5	36.7	41.4	21.7	38.1
Scale-intensive	21.9	40.0	37.9	47.8	38.6
Specialized suppliers	9.4	17.8	20.7	21.7	17.8
Science-based	6.3	5.6	—	8.7	5.6
Total	100	100	100	100	100
Service businesses					
Know-technology intensity	%	%	%	%	%
Supplier-dominated	31.0	16.4	17.6	18.6	19.5
Physical networks	17.2	46.6	44.1	27.1	35.9
IC networks	17.2	1.4	5.9	10.2	7.2
KIBS firms	34.5	35.6	32.4	44.1	37.4
Total	100	100	100	100	100

Note: The detailed classification is adopted from Castaldi [2009].

in their RD capabilities, the sources of technology and the requirements of their customers. These characteristics raise another question of whether the knowledge-technology intensity of a firm affects innovation [Pavitt, 1984; Delmar *et al.*, 2003]. Table 2.3 sheds light on this question by presenting the knowledge-technology intensity of performance profiles.

When exploring the innovation performer profiles within the manufacturing businesses, it can be found that the supplier-dominated firms are over-represented within the Low Performers. These firms are characterized by poor internal RD activities, weak technological capabilities and their customers are very price-sensitive [cf. Pavitt, 1984]. In addition to the supplier-dominated firms, the Radical and Incremental Performers accommodate a high share of scale-intensive firms. They are production-intensive coordinators and producers characterized by the RD activities for serving mainly internal purposes. However, within the Radical Performers there is also a slight over-representation of the specialized suppliers. These firms are focused on developing product innovations and customer-specific solutions in close collaboration with their performance-intensive customers. Finally, the High Performers accommodate a high share of science-based firms. These firms make higher investments in the

RD activities for creating a combination of product and process innovations and for that reason they require highly skilled employees in engineering and technology [cf. Pavitt, 1984; Hansen and Serin, 1997].

Correspondingly, when examining the performer profiles within the service businesses (see the bottom part of Table 2.3), it can be identified that they show several similarities with the manufacturing businesses. The supplier-dominated service providers are over-represented within the Low Performers. They are characterized by weak internal RD activities and low knowledge-technology intensity. These small firms offer personal and social services for local customers. On the other hand, the Low Performers accommodate a high share of firms specialized in IC networks being highly dependent on the applications of information and communication technology.

The firms of scale-intensive physical networks have an over-representation among both the Incremental and Radical Performers. These firms are characterized by the simplification of tasks and the large-scale processes. Finally, the knowledge-intensive business service (KIBS) providers are over-represented among the High Performers. These firms allocate a substantial amount of resources on the RD activities and they produce services by using efficiently the information and communication technologies. However, the share of the firms characterized by high knowledge-technology intensity is quite high also within the other profiles. [cf. Miozzo and Soete, 2001.]

Based on the above, it can be concluded that within the manufacturing businesses knowledge-technology intensity increases while the performer profile shifts from the Low Performer through the Incremental or Radical Performer towards the High Performer. Instead, within the service businesses the association between the innovation performer profile and knowledge-technology intensity is not so clear.

Regarding the age of firm, it has been commonly argued that the younger firms are more innovation-oriented than the older firms [Huergo and Jaumandreu, 2004]. On the other hand, Withers *et al.* [2011] found that age is associated with the capabilities to innovate. They explain that the capabilities needed to innovate accrue over time through cumulative learning and, for that reason the older firms may obtain higher outputs from their capabilities.

Table 2.4.   Age and size of firm by the innovation performer profile.

	Low Performer	Incremental Performer	Radical Performer	High Performer	Total
Manufacturing businesses	M	M	M	M	M
Age in 2003	15.8	13.6	10.4	15.0	13.8
Firm size in 2003–2004	14.2	12.0	15.7	14.2	13.6
Firm size in 2011–2012	12.1	14.4	18.2	21.4	16.2
Service businesses					
Age in 2003	11.8	11.6	6.7	10.3	10.4
Firm size in 2003–2004	7.4	3.7	4.5	5.7	5.3
Firm size in 2011–2012	6.9	7.5	4.0	10.5	7.3

Note: Firm size in terms of the calculatory number of employees.

When looking at the age of firms by performer profiles (see Table 2.4), it can be noticed that within both the manufacturing and service businesses, the Radical Performers are the youngest and the Low Performers are the oldest. This gives some support to the studies implying that the younger firms tend to show higher innovative probabilities [e.g., Huergo and Jaumandreu, 2004]. However, based on this empirical evidence, the young age is associated more strongly with the radical innovation activities but not with the incremental activities nor with the diversified innovation activities. The mean age of the Incremental and High Performers is above or close to average within both sectors. In the light of the above results, it seems that among the High and Incremental Performers the age of firm may result in positive effects through learning while among the Low Performers it may result in negative effects through obsolescence [cf. Nichter and Goldmark, 2009].

While the relationship between innovation and the age of firm is quite clear, the relationship between innovation and the size of firm has remained quite unclear. The general viewpoint seems to be that the increasing size of a firm leads to increased bureaucracy and structural inertia inhibiting innovation [cf. Dobbs and Hamilton, 2007]. However, it is challenging to conclude the direction of impact. The firm size may affect innovation or vice versa, innovation may result in growth affecting the size of firm.

When comparing small firms with large ones, the studies argue that the small size is associated with less innovation resulting in a conclusion that the small size tends to hinder innovation [Huergo and Jaumandreu, 2004; Plehn-Dujowich, 2009]. However, Bertschek and Entorf [1996] point out that the relationship between innovation and firm size is not linear. According to them, small and large firms are more innovative than the firms of intermediate size. Also Forsman and Rantanen [2011] identified that among the small firms with fewer than 50 employees the relationship between the size of firm and the innovative activities is not linear. They recognized that the size categories with five to nine employees and from 20 to 49 employees have more often developed incremental innovations than the other firms. Regarding the radical innovation activities, the manufacturing businesses with 20 to 49 employees have developed radical innovations more often than the other size categories. Instead, within the service businesses the smallest firms with fewer than 20 employees have more often developed radical innovations.

As regards the empirical evidence used in this book, Table 2.4 presents the size of firm for the period of 2003–2004 and again for the period of 2011–2012 by the innovation performer profiles. As can be seen, the manufacturing businesses are larger in size than the service businesses. When looking at the changes in the firm size across the performer profiles, some dramatic differences can be located. At the beginning of the examination period in 2003–2004, the Radical Performers have the largest average size within the manufacturing businesses. Eight years later, in 2011–2012 the situation has changed. The High Performers have grown very fast bypassing in size the Radical Performers. Correspondingly, within the service businesses, the Low Performers are the largest firms in 2003–2004. However, in 2011–2012, the High Performers, due to their very rapid growth, have bypassed the Low Performers in terms of size.

As mentioned earlier, it is difficult to conclude whether the size of firm affects innovation or the other way around — whether innovation results in growth affecting the size of firm [cf. Delmar *et al.*, 2003]. In order to explore the changes in firm size, the progress is illustrated along with a period of 10 years from 2003 to 2012. This examination includes only the survivor firms. Hence, the firms that have experienced bankruptcy or the termination of business activities are excluded. It should be noted that the highest share of such firms were located among the Radical Performers (15.9%) and the Low Performers (13.1%) while 8.6% of the Incremental Performers and only 5.7% of the High Performers have experienced the discontinuation of their business operations.

Figure 2.5 illustrates how the average size of a firm has changed within the manufacturing and service businesses. As can be seen, all four profiles within the manufacturing businesses started to expand smoothly lasting until 2007–2008. In 2008 and 2009, the economy encountered an unforeseen and dramatic recession. Within the manufacturing businesses, economic downturn affected especially the Incremental and Radical Performers by turning an expansion into a decline. In 2011, the manufacturing businesses started a slow recovery. Compared to the firm size in 2003–2004, the High Performers experienced a prominent expansion during the period of 10 years while the Incremental and Radical Performers are slightly above the level in which they started at the beginning of the examination period. Instead, the Low Performers are below the level they were in 2003–2004.

Correspondingly, when exploring the firm size within the service businesses, it can be noticed that the Incremental Performers started with a rapid expansion in 2005 while the Radical and High Performers had a smoother progress (see Figure 2.5, bottom part). They grew in size during the favorable economic climate until 2007–2008. Confronted with the recession in 2009, the Radical Performers started to decline while the High Performers recovered quit easily and continued their steady expansion. Despite recession, the Incremental Performers were able to stabilize their size. Instead, the Radical Performers are in the declining progress. In 2011–2012, they are still below the size they were ten years ago in 2003–2004. Finally, during the period of 10 years the Low Performers have been quite stable in size.

It can be concluded that within the survivor firms, the High and Incremental Performers have possessed the most promising trend during the period of 10 years. It also seems that these firms have been less vulnerable to the economic downturn measured by the calculatory number of employees. Hence, this result suggests that the incremental and diversified

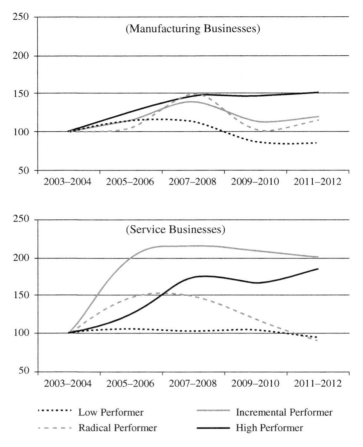

Fig. 2.5.   Changes in firm size within the manufacturing and service businesses.

innovation activities may be an important condition for transforming the economic crisis into an opportunity. Correspondingly, the Radical and Low Performers have been the most vulnerable to the economic downturn. However, within the manufacturing businesses they started a smooth recovery in 2010 while within the service businesses the Radical Performers have not been able to turn their declining trend into an expansion.

In general, these patterns give a reason to assume that the diversity of innovation activities are associated with the size of firm. In addition, the patterns suggest that the most promising long-term growth in terms of number of employees can be found among the High Performers of the manufacturing businesses and the High and Incremental Performers within the service businesses. The Radical Performers have highest fluctuation in their size and the Low Performers are characterized by stable or declining size. However, the growth processes of small firms will be explored in more detail in Chapter 4.

2.6 Chapter Summary

The aim of this chapter was to provide a comprehensive view of innovation activities in small firms. It started by exploring what kinds of innovations are typical in small firms. In this book innovation is considered broadly as both the development and commercial phenomenon. This stance emphasizes that the resource-scarce small firms should strive to the speedy development and commercialization of innovations.

By adopting a broad definition of innovation, the empirical evidence used in this book reveals that 9 out of 10 small firms are innovators. Instead, if innovation is limited to those that represent a high degree of newness, only 4 firms out of 10 are innovators. Hence, the small firms tend to favor the incremental innovation activities. If the diversity of innovation activities is low, these firms typically make incremental improvements to their current products and services. The share of process innovations increases while the innovation activities diversify. The product innovations are also the typical outcomes of the radical innovation activities, especially within the service businesses. Instead, the radical process innovations are infrequently reported outcomes reflecting that small firms are slow to implement radical internal change.

Although the findings of this book regarding the dominant innovation types in small firms are somewhat conflicting with the prior studies, they demonstrate, however, in line with prior literature that innovation patterns are as diversified in the service businesses as they are in manufacturing businesses [Evangelista, 2000; de Jong and Marsili, 2006; Forsman, 2011].

Nevertheless, the above commonly used approach to explore only single innovations has been criticized for resulting in a static snapshot of innovation in small firms. Several scholars have suggested that in order to be successful over a longer period of time, small firms should have diversified activities for generating a continuous stream of innovative outcomes. In order to capture a more dynamic picture of innovation in small firms, the focus was shifted from the innovations of small firms on the small firms as innovators. In order to examine the characteristics of different kinds of innovators, an innovation performer profile was specified to every firm based on the history of innovation activities.

Four divergent profiles emerge from the empirical evidence: Low Performers, Incremental Performers, Radical Performers and High Performers. By combining the results of the empirical evidence collected for this book and the characteristics of the model developed by Boly *et al.* [2014] within the French firms, a more comprehensive picture of innovation patterns across the different kinds of innovators was captured. Table 2.5 summarizes these patterns.

Table 2.5.   Summary of the innovation patterns by innovation performer profiles.

	Low Performer	**Incremental Performer**	**Radical Performer**	**High Performer**
Innovation patterns				
Future orientation	Defensive	Short-term	Medium-term	Longer term
Approach to change	Passive	Reactive	Pro/reactive	Proactive
Innovation management practices	Weak or non-existent	Weak	Varies	Strong
Innovation activities	Non-existent or incremental	Incremental	Radical	Radical and incremental
Innovation regularity	Infrequent	Occasional	Occasional	Continuous
Innovation diversity	Very low	Low	Low	High
Business environment-related factors[a]				
Location (Urban/Rural)	Varies	SER more urban	SER more urban	MAN more rural
Firm satisfaction	Neutral	Neutral	Low in SER	High in SER Low in MAN
Employee satisfaction	Low	Neutral	Low in SER	High
Regional services	Low	Average	High in MAN Low in SER	High in SER
Firm-related factors				
Knowledge-technology intensity	Low	Varies	Varies	Medium to high
Trend in size of firm	Decline	Growth	Fluctuating	Growth

Note: [a]MAN = manufacturing businesses and SER = service businesses.

Low Performers — These firms are non-innovators that rely on their current products and processes. They are slow to respond to changes. Only occasionally these firms make minor improvements to their products and services. The Low Performers are passive firms with a short-term vision and defensive strategy and they tend to neglect the innovation management practices. These firms are located within the sectors characterized by low knowledge-technology intensity, weak internal RD, price-sensitive customers and standardized products. It is natural that these firms are the unusual customers of regional development and consultancy services. While the owner-managers are quite satisfied to their business environment, the employees are less satisfied to their living and working environment. The size of the Low Performers has a declining trend.

Incremental Performers — These firms are inclined to react to the changes in their business environment by making incremental improvements in the current products and services. These reactive firms are occasional innovators with low innovation diversity, short-term vision and quite poor innovation management practices. The Incremental Performers are more entrepreneurial than innovative. They are located in the production-intensive sectors characterized by low or medium knowledge-technology intensity, relatively low investments allocated in the RD activities and price-sensitive customers. However, the Incremental Performers accommodate a quite high share of KIBS. What comes to the business environment, these firms are neutral regarding satisfaction as well as regional services. Finally, their size has a growing trend.

Radical Performers — They are quite dynamic firms that anticipate changes and respond to them by developing radically new products and services. While the degree of novelty is high, the diversity of innovation activities is low. These firms have a medium-term vision, an emphasis on technology, competences and project management. Their innovation process is operating but the organization of activities is weaker. Somewhat surprisingly, their knowledge-technology intensity does not differ significantly from Incremental Performers. In regard to the business environment-related issues, satisfaction is low within the service businesses and neutral within the manufacturing businesses. While the use of regional services is quite high within the manufacturing businesses, it is relatively low within the service businesses. Finally, the size of the Radical Performers is fluctuating.

High Performers — These dynamic firms are continuous innovators characterized by high diversity in their innovation activities. The high Performers have a longer term vision, proactive approach to changes and strong innovation management practices. Change is visible in these firms. They are engaged in implementing both incremental and radical changes in their products and services as well as in their processes for producing and delivering these offerings. The High Performers accommodate the highest share of high knowledge-technology firms characterized by significant investments in RD, performance-sensitive customers and dynamic learning. Satisfaction to the business environment is low within the manufacturing businesses while it is high within service businesses. The service businesses seem also to be more regular customers of regional development services. The size of these firms has a growing trend.

In summary, this chapter deepened the understanding of innovation in small firms by creating an elaborate view of their innovation activities. It also illustrated what kinds of innovators small firms are. However, it did not identify the potential drivers that stimulate small firms to innovate. This issue will be addressed in the next chapter. It focuses on the input-based factors for exploring the innovation capacity of small firms.

References

Amable, B. and Palombarini, S. (1998). Technical change and incorporated R&D in the service sector, *Research Policy*, 27(7), pp. 655–675.

Amara, N., Landry, R. and Doloreux, D. (2009). Patterns of innovation in knowledge intensive business services, *The Service Industries Journal*, 29(4), pp. 407–430.

Ambec, S. and Lanoie, P. (2008). Does it pay to be green? A systematic overview, *Academy of Management Perspectives*, 22(4), pp. 45–62.

Ateljevic, J. and Doorne, S. (2004). Diseconomies of scale: A study of development constraints in small tourism firms in central New Zealand, *Tourism and Hospitality Research*, 5(1), pp. 5–24.

Aubert, J-E. (2005). *Promoting Innovation in Developing Countries: A Conceptual Framework*. World Bank Policy Research Working Papers 3554. Online. Available at: http://elibrary.worldbank.org/doi/book/10.1596/1813-9450-3554 (Accessed 16.06.2014).

Avermaete, T., Viaene, J., Morgan, E.J. and Crawford, N. (2003). Determinants of innovation in small food firms, *European Journal of Innovation Management*, 6(1), pp. 8–17.

Bertschek, I. and Entorf, H. (1996). On nonparametric estimation of the Schumpeterian link between innovation and firm size: Evidence from Belgium, France and Germany, *Empirical Economics*, 21(3), pp. 401–426.

Bessant, J., Lamming, R., Noke, H. and Phillips, W. (2005). Managing innovation beyond the steady state, *Technovation*, 25(12), pp. 1366–1376.

Boly, V., Morel, L., Assielou, N.G. and Camargo, M. (2014). Evaluating innovative processes in French firms: Methodological proposition for firm innovation capacity evaluation, *Research Policy*, 43(3), pp. 608–622.

Castaldi, C. (2009). The relative weight of manufacturing and services in Europe: An innovation perspective, *Technological Forecasting & Social Change*, 76(6), pp. 709–722.

Cohen, W.M. and Klepper, S. (1996). A reprise of size and R&D, *The Economic Journal*, 106(437), pp. 925–951.

Dahlin, K.B. and Behrens, D.M. (2005). When is an invention really radical? Defining and measuring technological radicalness, *Research Policy*, 34(5), pp. 717–737.

Damanpour, F. (1996). Organizational complexity and innovation: Developing and testing multiple contingency models, *Management Science*, 42(5), pp. 693–716.

Damanpour, F. and Aravind, D. (2012). Managerial innovation: Conceptions, processes, and antecedents, *Management and Organization Review*, 8(2), pp. 423–454.

Damanpour, F. and Gopalakrishnan, S. (2001). The dynamics of the adoption of product and process innovations in organizations, *Journal of Management Studies*, 38(1), pp. 45–65.

Damanpour, F., Walker, R.M. and Avellaneda, C.N. (2009). Combinative effects of innovation types and organizational performance: A longitudinal study of service organizations, *Journal of Management Studies*, 46(4), pp. 650–675.

Damanpour, F. and Wischnevsky, J.D. (2006). Research on innovation in organizations: Distinguishing innovation-generating from innovation-adopting organizations, *Journal of Engineering and Technology Management*, 23(4), pp. 269–291.

de Jong, J.P.J. and Marsili, O. (2006). The fruit flies of innovations: A taxonomy of innovative small firms, *Research Policy*, 35(2), pp. 213–229.

de Jong, J.P.J. and Vermeulen, P.A.M. (2006). Determinants of product innovation in small firms, *International Small Business Journal*, 24(6), pp. 587–609.

Delmar, F., Davidsson, P. and Gartner, W.B. (2003). Arriving at high-growth firm, *Journal of Business Venturing*, 18(2), pp.189–216.

Dewar, R.D. and Dutton, J.E. (1986). The adoption of radical and incremental innovations: An empirical analysis, *Management Science*, 32(11), pp. 1422–1433.

Dobbs, M. and Hamilton, R.T. (2007). Small business growth: Recent evidence and new directions, *International Journal of Entrepreneurial Behaviour & Research*, 13(5), pp. 296–322.

Ellonen, H-K., Wikström, P. and Jantunen, A. (2009). Linking dynamic-capability portfolios and innovation outcomes, *Technovation*, 29(11), pp. 753–762.

Estrin, S., Korosteleva, J. and Mickiewicz, T. (2013). Which institutions encourage entrepreneurial growth aspirations? *Journal of Business Venturing*, 28(4), pp. 564–580.

Evangelista, R. (2000). Sectoral patterns of technological change in services, *Economics of Innovation and New Technology*, 9(3), pp. 183–222.

Forsman, H. (2008). Business development success in SMEs: A case study approach, *Journal of Small Business and Enterprise Development*, 15(3), pp. 606–622.

Forsman, H. (2011). Innovation capacity and innovation development in small enterprises. A comparison between the manufacturing and service sectors, *Research Policy*, 40(5), pp. 739–750.

Forsman, H. and Annala, U. (2011). Small enterprises as innovators: Shift from a low performer to a high performer, *International Journal of Technology Management*, 56(2–4), pp. 154–171.

Forsman, H. and Rantanen, H. (2011). Small manufacturing and service enterprises as innovators: A comparison by size, *European Journal of Innovation Management*, 14(1), pp. 27–50.

Forsman, H. and Temel, S. (2011). Innovation and business performance in small enterprises. An enterprise-level analysis, *International Journal of Innovation Management*, 15(3), pp. 641–665

Forsman, H. and Temel, S. (2014). From a non-innovator to a high innovation performer: Networking as a driver. *Regional Studies* (in press).

Freel, M. (2005). The characteristics of innovation-intensive small firms: Evidence from "Northern Britain", *International Journal of Innovation Management*, 9(4), pp. 401–429.

Galindo, A.J. and Micco, A. (2007). Creditor protection and credit response to shocks, *World Bank Economic Review*, 21(3), pp. 413–438.

Garcia, R. and Calantone, R. (2002). A critical look at technological innovation typology and innovativeness terminology: A literature review, *Journal of Product Innovation Management*, 19(2), pp. 110–132.

Hansen, P.A. and Serin, G. (1997). Will low technology products disappear? The hidden innovation processes in low technology industries, *Technological Forecasting and Social Change*, 55(2), pp. 179–191.

Hirsch-Kreinsen, H. (2008). "Low-tech" innovations, *Industry and Innovation*, 15(1), pp. 19–43.

Horbach, J. (2008). Determinants of environmental innovation — New evidence from German Panel data sources, *Research Policy*, 37(1), pp. 163–173.

Huergo, E. and Jaumandreu, J. (2004). How does probability of innovation change with firm age, *Small Business Economics*, 22(3–4), pp. 193–207.

Johannessen, J-A., Olsen, B. and Lumpkin, G.T. (2001). Innovation as newness: What is new, how new, and new to whom? *European Journal of Innovation Management*, 4(1), pp. 20–31.

Kasmire, J., Korhonen, J.M. and Nikolic, I. (2012). How radical is a radical innovation? An outline for a computational approach, *Energy Procedia*, 20, pp. 346–353.

Kirner, E., Kinkel, S. and Jaeger, A. (2009). Innovation paths and the innovation performance of low-technology firms — an empirical analysis of German industry, *Research Policy*, 38(3), pp. 447–458.

Liedholm, C. (2002). Small firm dynamics: Evidence from Africa and Latin America, *Small Business Economics*, 18(1–3), pp. 225–240.

Miozzo, M. and Soete, L. (2001). Internationalization of services: A technological perspective, *Technological Forecasting and Social Science*, 67(2), pp. 159–185.

Nichter, S. and Goldmark, L. (2009). Small firm growth in developing countries, *World Development*, 37(9), pp. 1453–1464.

Nieto, M.J. and Santamaría, L. (2010). Technological collaboration: Bridging the innovation gap between small and large firms, *Journal of Small Business Management*, 48(1), pp. 44–69.

OECD (2005). *Oslo Manual, Guidelines for Collecting and Interpreting Innovation Data*, (A joint publication of OECD and Eurostat). Online. Available at: http://www.oecd.org/science/inno/2367580.pdf (Accessed 14.02.2015).

Pavitt, K. (1984). Sectoral patterns of technical change: Towards a taxonomy and a theory, *Research Policy*, 13(6), pp. 343–373.

Plehn-Dujowich, J.M. (2009). Firm size and types of innovation, *Economics of Innovation and New Technology*, 18(3), pp. 205–223.

Roberts, P.W. and Amit, R. (2003). The dynamics of innovative activity and competitive advantage: The case of Australian retail banking 1981 to 1995, *Organisation Science*, 14(2), pp. 107–122.

Robson, P.J.A. and Obeng, B.A. (2008). The barriers to growth in Ghana, *Small Business Economics*, 30(4), pp. 385–403.

Salazar, M. and Holbrook, A. (2004). A debate on innovation surveys, *Science and Public Policy*, 31(4), pp. 254–266.

Scozzi, B., Garavelli, C. and Crowston, K. (2005). Methods for modeling and supporting innovation processes in SMEs, *European Journal of Innovation Management*, 8(1), pp. 120–137.

Tushman, M.L. and O'Reilly III, C.A. (1996). Ambidextrous organizations: Managing evolutionary and revolutionary change, *California Management Review*, 38(4), pp. 8–30.

Verhees, F.J.H.M., Meulenberg, M.T.G. and Pennings, J.M.E. (2010). Performance expectations of small firms considering radical product innovation, *Journal of Business Research*, 63(7), pp. 772–777.

Withers, M.C., Drnevich, P.L. and Marino, L. (2011). Doing more with less: The disordinal implications of firm age for leveraging capabilities for innovation activity, *Journal of Small Business Management*, 49(4), pp. 515–536.

World Bank (2005). *Regulation and Taxation*. In *World Development Report*. (World Bank, Washington, DC).

Chapter 3

The Capacity of Small Firms to Innovate

3.1 Introduction

Innovation capacity has often been equated with internal resources allocated to formal RD activities. However, in small firms innovations are only seldom the results of planned activities characterized by scientific or technological knowledge. For example, de Jong and Marsili [2006] have identified that only one third of small firms have a formal plan for innovation. Instead, in smaller firms the innovation activities are integrated into their daily business operations [Forsman, 2008; Hirsch-Kreinsen, 2008; Kirner *et al.*, 2009]. Thus, as mentioned in the previous chapter, innovation can even be hidden to the innovators themselves [Hansen and Serin, 1997].

In such a situation, a healthy economic record is an important factor in enabling firms to allocate and acquire the adequate resources needed for innovation. Therefore, the prior business success of a firm may reflect its capacity to allocate internal resources for innovation [Davidsson *et al.*, 2009; Forsman *et al.*, 2013]. However, the resources alone are not enough for innovation. The firms need to possess a set of capabilities for utilizing these resources efficiently. Accordingly, the resource-based view summarizes that the innovation capacity of a firm consists of a bundle of resources and capabilities that together contribute to the achievement of successful innovation. The resources are the assets that a firm controls while the capabilities are the abilities of a firm to exploit these resources [Helfat and Peteraf, 2003]. This capacity can be enhanced by acquiring external knowledge and other resources through business collaboration.

This chapter explores the above three items of innovation capacity: the internal resources allocated to innovation activities, the capabilities needed to exploit these resources and the external capacity acquired through networking. In addition, the capacity requirements along with the journey from the Low Performer to the High Performer are illustrated.

3.2 Internal Resources to Innovate

Although small firms typically have resource constraints, they are often successful innovators. Nevertheless, in the case that innovations are developed internally, adequate resources should be allocated to innovation activities. For example, Rosenbusch *et al.* [2011] found that internally derived investments in innovation activities are beneficial for small firms especially if these innovations are radical in nature. They continue that the internal innovation projects might foster the creation of innovation capabilities, could speed up the completion of innovation projects and might allow a full appropriation of the returns from the innovation projects. However, previous studies predominantly present contradictory findings leading to the proposition that the requirements to collaborate increase while the degree of novelty of innovation increases [cf. Freel and Harrison, 2006; Rosenbusch *et al.*, 2011].

Thus, prior literature submits conflicting recommendations whether or not small firms should organize their innovation activities internally or engage in the collaborative endeavors with their business partners. Table 3.1 shows how the sample of small firms used in this book have allocated resources in the internal RD activities. This information has been converted from categorized data. The original values are presented in Appendix.

As can be noticed, within both the manufacturing and service businesses the investments in RD activities increase while the innovation performer profile shifts from the Low Performer towards the High Performer. The majority of the Low and Incremental Performers have

Table 3.1.   Internal resources by innovation performer profile.

	Low Performer %	Incremental Performer %	Radical Performer %	High Performer %	Total %
Manufacturing businesses					
Input to RD activities					
Percentage of sales[a]	0.4	1.0	1.9	2.4	1.4
Do not know[b]	18.8	6.7	13.8	2.2	8.6
Abilities to finance hidden innovation	Low	High	Very low	Very high	—
Service businesses					
Input to RD activities					
Percentage of sales[a]	0.6	1.1	2.1	2.6	1.7
Do not know[b]	13.8	23.3	11.8	1.7	13.3
Abilities to finance hidden innovation	Low	Above average	Below average	Above average	—

Notes: [a]Converted from categorized data, original values are provided in Appendix, Table A3.2.
[b]Percentage of firms that do not know their input to RD activities.

allocated less than 2% of their sales to the RD activities while the Radical and High Performers report about higher allocations. Hence, it can be concluded that the firms with radical innovation activities have more commonly allocated the separate resources for RD activities. Instead, the above results reflect that the incremental innovation activities will more commonly take place integrated into the daily business operations of small firms.

Nevertheless, there exist differences between the absolute and relative values. Due to the fact that the absolute value of sales is higher within the manufacturing businesses, also the absolute value of their investments is higher than within the service businesses. Hence, the relative input to RD activities is higher within the service businesses while the absolute input is higher within the manufacturing businesses.

de Jong and Marsili [2006] have identified that only one half of small firms reserve a separate budget for innovation. This could be one reason for the difficulties in assessing the value of resources allocated to the innovation activities. In this data, 11% of the respondents could not express the share of sales invested in RD activities. Within the manufacturing businesses the largest share of these firms can be located among the Low Performers while within the service businesses, the Incremental Performers have most often reported that they do not know the level of their RD investments.

When innovations are developed beside the daily business operations and being even hidden in nature, a logical question is whether this results in extra costs and if yes, whether small firms could afford such activities. One answer can be found in their cash and profit figures. It can be assumed that a wealthy firm may have better abilities to hidden innovation than its indigent counterpart. By using these as indicators, the Incremental and High Performers have the best abilities to finance their hidden innovation (see Table 3.1). Instead, especially among the manufacturing businesses, both the Low and Radical Performers may face difficulties in these hidden activities.

However, as mentioned earlier, the capacity to allocate resources is not enough alone. It is needed to possess the abilities to integrate, build, and reconfigure these resources [Barney, 1991; Szeto, 2000; Zott, 2003]. Thus, while the resources reflect the stocks of available factors that are controlled by a firm, the capabilities reflect the abilities to transform these resources for meeting the innovation goals of a firm [Amit and Schoemaker, 1993]. The next section explores these capabilities.

3.3 Capabilities to Innovate

The dynamic capabilities and absorptive capacity are the two commonly used frameworks to predict successful innovation. The former, absorptive capacity reflects the ability of a firm to learn from others. It has been encapsulated as an ability of a firm to recognize the value of new external knowledge, to assimilate and transform it to the commercial means [Cohen and Levinthal, 1990]. Hence, four distinct areas can be identified for absorptive capacity: acquisition, assimilation, transformation and exploitation. Acquisition refers to the capabilities to identify and acquire external knowledge that is critical for a firm while assimilation refers to the capabilities of a firm to analyze, process, interpret and understand the acquired external knowledge. Transformation reflects the abilities of a firm to develop and refine its processes and procedures that facilitate the integration of acquired new external knowledge with current knowledge. Finally, exploitation refers to the abilities of a firm to exploit the new knowledge. [Cohen and Levinthal, 1990; Zahra and George, 2002.]

According to Zahra and George [2002], acquisition and assimilation reflect potential absorptive capacity while transformation and exploitation reflect realized absorptive capacity. These two concepts have separate but complementary functions for improving the performance of firms. The firms cannot exploit and create value with knowledge without first exploring and acquiring it. Correspondingly, without the abilities to transform and exploit acquired knowledge for profit generation, the value of new knowledge is scant.

Absorptive capacity relies on two components: the current knowledge-base created through the past activities and the efforts made to acquire and exploit new external knowledge [Caloghirou *et al.*, 2004; Hurmelinna-Laukkanen and Olander, 2014]. The degree of current knowledge plays an important role in knowledge absorption. The lack of appropriate prior knowledge leads to a cognitive barrier. In small firms it can be a major challenge due to the fact that a firm may not be able to internalize and exploit complicated external knowledge if its current knowledge is at low level [cf. Jones *et al.*, 2010]. Hence, a firm may be better equipped to accumulate new knowledge if it already has developed some absorptive capacity in this particular field [Cohen and Levinthal, 1990].

The fact how a small firm can adapt to its business environment and exploit the opportunities it offers depends very much on the knowledge and capabilities of its owner-managers and employees [Chan *et al.*, 2006]. Thus, these individuals who often through learning by doing accumulate their knowledge are the key actors in the innovation activities of small firms [Hansen and Serin, 1997]. In addition, the goals of owner-managers are crucial for directing the activities to learn and innovate [cf. Gray, 2006; Jones *et al.*, 2010].

Nevertheless, Cohen and Levinthal [1990] point out that while the absorptive capacity of a firm depends on the capacities of its owner-manager and employees, at a firm-level it is not simply the sum of the absorptive capacities of its individual members. Learning and knowledge creation must be institutionalized in systems, processes and routines [Jones *et al.*, 2010]. These internal mechanisms of a firm affect not only the acquisition and assimilation of knowledge but also the exploitation of it.

In small firms, absorptive capacity is more likely to be developed as a byproduct of the daily business activities in a situation in which new acquired knowledge is closely related to the current knowledge base. Whenever a small firm aims to acquire and use knowledge that is unrelated to its current knowledge base, it must dedicate in improving significantly its absorptive capacity. [Cohen and Levinthal, 1990.]

While Cohen and Levinthal [1990] discussed on absorptive capacity mainly as a firm-level concept, Lane and Lubatkin [1998] enhanced it by exploring how firms can develop their capabilities by acquiring knowledge from other firms. Learning from others addresses the need of firms to continuously adapt, reconfigure and develop their capabilities. This builds a bridge to another commonly used framework, the dynamic capabilities of a firm. It consists of sensing and shaping new opportunities, seizing these opportunities, and orchestrating and reconfiguring the intangible and tangible assets of a firm for maintaining its competitiveness [cf. Teece, 2007; Branzei and Vertinsky, 2006].

Sensing refers to the capabilities of a firm to constantly search and explore relevant intelligence from local and global sources about consumer expectations, competitor activities and technological possibilities. Once the new opportunities are sensed, they must be addressed through new products, processes or services. This demands answers not only to the when and where questions but firms must also answer the how question. This should be done by creating an appropriate business model that defines how value is created and captured. Teece [2007] warns that in the short-term the successful business model may breed some level of routine that is needed for operational efficiency. However, a key to long-term success is the ability of a firm to reconfigure its assets, processes and structures for responding to the changes in its business environment.

In a similar vein as with absorptive capacity [Zahra and George, 2002], also the dynamic capabilities are associated with two functions: exploration and exploitation [March, 1991]. Dixon *et al.* [2014] have identified that exploration together with path creation are the prerequisites for developing the unique capabilities while exploitation accompanied with the deployment of current knowledge are the prerequisites for developing the operational capabilities. Hence, while exploration and path creation enable firms to renew their abilities for responding to the changes in their business environment, the operational capabilities facilitate the efficient use of existing resources for running today's business operations [Zahra *et al.*, 2006; Winter, 2003].

However, these two types of capabilities are in a virtuous interaction supporting the firms that simultaneously pursue the exploration and exploitation activities [Dixon *et al.*, 2014]. Also March [1991] highlights that these two capabilities should be in balance. Thus, in order to explore the potential future business opportunities the firms should be able to allocate their resources for developing new capabilities. They must also be capable to efficiently improve their current capabilities for exploiting today's business opportunities [Raisch *et al.*, 2009].

In small firms the exploration and exploitation activities compete for the same scarce resources. Due to the fact that the returns from the exploration activities are uncertain and distant accompanied by high risks, small firms are inclined to increase the reliability of returns through the exploitation activities [March, 1991]. While this one-sided emphasis on the exploitation activities may result in higher short-term profits, it may also result in a competence trap [Raisch *et al.*, 2009]. In such a situation a small firm is not able to respond to the changes in its business environment. On the contrary, if the high emphasis on the exploration activities drives out the exploitation activities, it may improve the ability of a firm to renew its capabilities, but it may also result in an unrewarding change and failure trap [March, 1991; Raisch *et al.*, 2009].

In small firms the risk-propensity affects how the exploitation and exploration activities are balanced. For example, Herrmann *et al.* [2007] point out that the willingness to take risks is essential for radical innovation development. However, high risk-propensity should be accompanied by the capabilities to manage these risks. Nicholas *et al.* [2013] emphasize that small firms often use the probe and learn strategy reflecting the fact that they make decisions incrementally in smaller steps as the idea develops. This may be one way to manage the risks of radical innovation activities.

By combining the frameworks of absorptive capacity and dynamic capabilities, the capabilities of small firms are explored in this book based on four dimensions.

First, the abilities of firms to acquire and assimilate external knowledge have been titled as knowledge acquisition. This dimension refers to potential absorptive capacity [cf. Zahra and George, 2002]. Directed by the concept of dynamic capabilities, the realized absorptive capacity has been divided into two dimensions: exploitation and exploration capabilities.

The second dimension, entitled as exploitation capabilities, consists of the capabilities to transform acquired and assimilated knowledge into improvements in the existing offerings and the capabilities of firms to exploit them by having emphasis on their current customers. These more or less operational capabilities reflect the abilities of firms to exploit today's business opportunities.

However, Danneels [2002] points out that the firms should not solely focus on their existing customer base but also devote to exploring new potential markets. Accordingly, the capabilities to transform acquired and assimilated knowledge into the radically new offerings and exploit them by having emphasis on the new customer segments have been entitled as the exploration capabilities. This third dimension reflects the abilities of firms to exploit their future business opportunities.

Finally, high risk-propensity has been connected especially with the exploration activities. Therefore, the risk management capabilities have been included in this examination. This fourth dimension comprises the capabilities to assess the risks, willingness to take the risks and the abilities to manage the risks. The items of the above four capability dimensions are presented in Appendix, Table A3.1.

Figures 3.1 and 3.2 illustrate how the small firms used as a sample in this book have assessed the status of their current capabilities. As can be seen, the capability curves reveal several similarities. In both manufacturing and service businesses the Low and Incremental Performers have assessed that their current capabilities are below average while the Radical and High Performers possess much higher values. In addition to this, within both sectors the Radical Performers have assessed the highest values for their current capabilities.

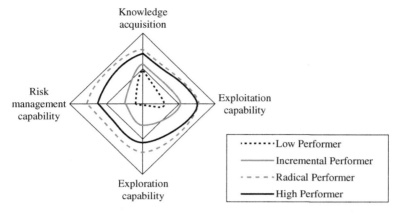

Fig. 3.1. Current capabilities assessed by the manufacturing businesses (perimeter is high, center is weak).

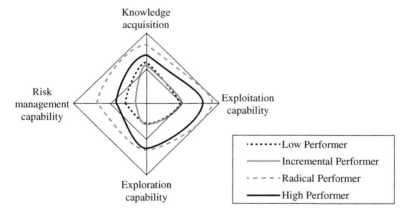

Fig. 3.2. Current capabilities assessed by the service businesses (perimeter is high, center is weak).

In general, the capability curves demonstrate that the status of current capabilities will strengthen while the innovation activities diversify. This supports the arguments that in small firms the capabilities are created through learning by doing integrated into the innovation activities. Especially the activities for developing the radically new innovations seem to demand the radical improvements in capabilities.

Instead, the capability curves of the Incremental Performers deviate from this reasoning. Although the Incremental Performers of the manufacturing businesses have higher values for all four capability dimensions than the Low Performers, the Incremental Performers of the service businesses seem to have even lower values than the Low Performers. This reflects the fact that the engagement in the incremental innovation activities does not demand as dramatic changes in the capabilities as are needed for developing radically new innovations. On the other hand, these capability curves reflect that the Low and Incremental Performers are inclined to increase their profits through the exploitation activities.

Correspondingly, also the Radical and High Performers share several similarities. In general, the current capabilities of these two performer profiles are at a higher level compared with the Low and Incremental Performers. In addition, they have recognized the importance of all four capability dimensions. Based on the current capability status, these firms possess a better balance between the exploration and exploitation activities.

While the current capabilities demonstrate the existing abilities of small firms, it is assumed that the importance of a capability dimension to a firm reflects its future goals. Table 3.2 presents the importance of each capability dimension by innovation performer profiles.

As can be noticed, the Low Performers within the manufacturing businesses differ from other profiles by their low importance values reflecting that in the future these firms intend to continue along with their conventional pathways. Instead, the Low Performers within the service businesses as well as the Incremental Performers within both sectors have realized a dramatic need for the improvements regarding the capabilities for knowledge acquisition, exploitation and exploration. These firms may have identified that they are approaching a competence trap and the situation in which they are not able to respond to the changes in their business environment. In order to avoid this, they must improve their exploration capabilities.

This, however, is challenging for many small firms due to the fact that they need to acquire and assimilate such knowledge that is unrelated to their current knowledge base. Cohen and Levinthal [1990] warn that this is a situation in which firms must dedicate efforts exclusively to creating

Table 3.2. The importance of capability dimensions by the innovation performer profiles.

	Low Performer M	Incremental Performer M	Radical Performer M	High Performer M	Total M
Manufacturing businesses					
Knowledge acquisition	0.25	0.46	0.39	0.60	0.45
Exploitation capability	0.31	0.45	0.43	0.57	0.45
Exploration capability	0.16	0.42	0.59	0.60	0.45
Risk management capability	−0.05	0.08	0.20	0.36	0.14
Service businesses					
Knowledge acquisition	0.44	0.44	0.66	0.48	0.49
Exploitation capability	0.39	0.41	0.53	0.47	0.45
Exploration capability	0.35	0.45	0.50	0.49	0.45
Risk management capability	0.07	0.00	0.33	0.15	0.11

Note: Scale: 1 = important, 0 = neutral and −1 = not important.

new knowledge with a risk that they should sacrifice their current profits. The Low and Incremental Performers do not have the ambitious goals for improving their relatively low risk management capabilities. This reflects that they are not ready for such risk taking that is required.

What comes to the Radical Performers, within the manufacturing businesses they have assessed the highest importance for exploration capabilities while within the service businesses they have assessed the highest importance for knowledge acquisition. Thus, the Radical Performers (especially within the manufacturing businesses) may approach the situation in which, through the exploration activities, they are able to renew their capabilities but the limited exploitation activities could lead to an imbalance with a risk of unrewarding change and failure trap.

Finally, the High Performers have assessed an almost equal importance of the capabilities for knowledge acquisition, exploitation and exploration. This indicates that the High Performers have balanced their goals for exploitation and exploration. Hence, they simultaneously pursue exploiting the current business opportunities as well as exploring the future business opportunities. Considering the innovation patterns of the High Performers, they are able to maintain their capabilities as a byproduct of their innovation activities. Based on the above, it can be summarized that the Low and Incremental Performers are biased towards the exploitation of their current business opportunities. However, the majority of them have realized the need for balancing the exploitation and exploration activities. Nevertheless, the low level of risk management capabilities may become a weakness for achieving the balance. Instead, the Radical Performers are inclined towards the exploration activities while they seem to have weaknesses in their exploitation activities. Finally, the High Performers seem to have balanced their capabilities for both exploitation and exploration.

One solution for small firms to overcome the above challenges is to establish collaboration with external parties for learning, getting access to external resources and sharing the risks. The question of how the capacity to innovate can be enhanced through collaboration will be discussed in the next section.

3.4 External Resources to Innovate

It has been commonly argued that in today's fast-changing business environment innovation is not anymore the domain of an individual firm. Instead, it is the matter of collaboration in networks [cf. Freel and Harrison, 2006]. Especially small firms can enhance their capacity to innovate through business networking [Szeto, 2000; Caniëls and Romijn, 2003; Forsman and Rantanen, 2011]. Traditionally collaboration has been considered useful for getting access to new resources and sharing risks. Due to the fact that competition has changed to being more knowledge-based, collaboration for learning has become even a more important goal of firms [Lane and Lubatkin, 1998]. By acquiring and exploiting knowledge developed by others, small firms can through the learning networks enhance their knowledge base and foster their capability creation. On the other hand, the capacity to exploit external new knowledge acquired through networking has been found to have a positive effect on the probability of being a successful innovator [de Faria *et al.*, 2010].

Thus, the balance between the exploitation and exploration activities may be created through the networking activities [Kauppila, 2010]. These activities can be formal or informal in nature. As regards the formal networks, the members jointly create them and give an access to new members while the informal networks emerge naturally as a result of even ad hoc interactions [Chetty and Agndal, 2008].

In small firms in which the owner-manager has a high impact on the innovation activities, one's informal interpersonal networks affect the activities [Shaw, 2006]. While the interpersonal relations can be even critical in importance for improving the daily activities, these activities often lead to a process in which the individual relationships become a part of the activities of the entire firm [Ettlinger, 2003; Shaw, 2006; Chetty and Agndal, 2008]. Jones *et al.* [2010] point out that the owner-managers of small firms should become aware of how they build their relationships for enhancing the capacity of the firm to innovate.

Small firms and their owner-managers make individual decisions to join business networks. There are a variety of theories that explain the motives for networking [cf. van Gils and Zwart, 2009] such as cost savings [Levine and White, 1961], savings in transaction costs [Williamson, 1992], the power to control the resource allocation [Pfeffer and Salancik, 2003], getting access to the pool of complementary resources [Eisenhardt and Schoonhoven, 1996] and knowledge as a critical source of competitive advantage [Grant and Baden-Fuller, 2004].

Nevertheless, van Gils and Zwart [2009] argue that in order to capture the different levels of motives there is a need for a balanced theoretical pluralism and thus, instead of striving only one theory, the researchers should examine where these approaches complement each other. Lin and Zhang [2005], who have adopted a pluralist approach for studying networking in SMEs, combine transaction cost with the strategic independence and resource-based views. Based on these frameworks, they have identified three types of motives for network formation: the motives to acquire and enhance the existing resources, the motives to improve efficiency by reducing and sharing costs and risks, and finally, the motives to strengthen competitive advantage and avert direct competition.

The above-mentioned motives to join the business networks reflect what the expected intangible and tangible benefits from networking are [Simon, 1997]. In fact, the small business owner-managers may consider several factors before entering into collaborative networks [van Gils and Zwart, 2009]. For example, they may want to enhance their knowledge, search for new business opportunities for getting access to new markets or they may want to improve their abilities to compete in the existing markets by lowering the costs [Smedlund, 2006; Öberg and Grundström, 2009]. Mazzarol and Reboud [2008] summarize that small firms collaborate for ensuring access to resources, facilitating business development, sustaining competitive advantage or boosting their business performance.

However, in order to maximize the benefits gained through collaboration, small firms must search for the right partners to build an optimal structure for their networks [Rowley *et al.*, 2000]. This is supported by Jiang *et al.* [2010] who point out that through the functional diversity the networking firms can build a balanced portfolio to strengthen not only their current viability through collaboration in the market-related and efficiency-related activities (exploitation) but also their future viability through collaboration in the development-related activities (exploration). In the development-related activities, learning plays a key role. Lane and Lubatkin [1998] point out that learning can be maximized by collaborating with such partners that have the similar basic knowledge base but the different specialized knowledge base.

The benefits gained through networking among the firms used as a sample in this book, are explored by having a focus on the development-related, efficiency-related and market-related activities. The development-related benefits gained through collaboration enhance the capacity of a firm to explore the potential future business opportunities while the efficiency-related and market-related benefits enhance the capacity to exploit today's business opportunities.

The above three types of benefits are the outcomes of formal networks. In addition to these, in small firms also the informal networks of owner-managers affect the activities [cf. Shaw, 2006]. Therefore, the benefits gained through socializing should be included in the examination. It is expected that these individual relationships become a part of the activities of a firm and thus, represent the potential new relationships that are transformed into interorganizational networks [Ettlinger, 2003; Shaw, 2006; Chetty and Agndal, 2008].

Table 3.3 presents how the small firms in the sample collected for this book have benefited through collaboration.

As can be noticed, the manufacturing businesses have reported most commonly about the networking benefits gained through development-related and efficiency-related collaboration while the service

Table 3.3.   Benefits gained through networking by the innovation performer profile.

	Low Performer M	**Incremental Performer M**	**Radical Performer M**	**High Performer M**	**Total M**
Manufacturing businesses					
Development-related	36.5	40.7	51.7	62.3	46.7
Market-related	32.3	37.0	39.1	50.0	39.6
Efficiency-related	25.0	47.8	50.0	47.8	44.4
Socializing	31.2	35.6	27.6	60.9	39.6
Service businesses					
Development-related	39.1	45.2	55.9	57.1	49.7
Market-related	31.0	46.1	36.3	54.2	44.6
Efficiency-related	24.1	33.6	13.2	39.8	30.5
Socializing	48.3	57.5	50.0	57.6	54.9

Note: Proportion of firms that have reported about the benefits in question.

businesses have reported most often about the benefits gained through socializing and the development-related activities. Another salient finding is that within the manufacturing businesses the networking benefits seem to accumulate while the innovation performer profile shifts from the Low Performer towards the High Performer. Instead, within the service businesses a similar pattern can be located only regarding the market-related activities. However, within both sectors the most striking differences can be found between the Low Performers and the High Performers. [cf. Forsman and Temel, 2014.]

According to Freel and Harrison [2006], the high degree of innovation novelty increases the requirements for networking. However, while they identified a significant positive association between networking and the novel innovations, they also recognized that approximately 50% of the incremental innovators and 30–40% of the novel innovators do not collaborate. The results of this study are in line with Freel and Harrison [2006] regarding the manufacturing sectors. The manufacturing businesses that have created the radical innovations with a high degree of novelty, have also more often than other firms benefited through networking. Instead, within the service businesses, the firms that have developed both incremental and radical innovations have reported more often than the other firms about the benefits gained through collaboration. Hence, it seems that the type of innovation affects networking within the manufacturing businesses while the diversity of developed innovations affects networking within the service businesses. The next section explores how the requirements of innovation capacity will change when the diversity of innovation activities increases.

3.5 Innovation Capacity as a Driver Towards the High Performer

An interesting question is how the requirements for innovation capacity will change along with the journey from the Low Performer to the High Performer. As explained in Section 2.3, there are two main routes. When proceeding along the first route, the Low Performer moves to the Incremental Performer by engaging in the incremental innovation activities. Thereafter, the firm expands its activities to cover also the radical innovation development, and it shifts from the Incremental Performer to the High Performer. In the case that the firm selects to proceed along with the second route, the Low Performer shifts to the Radical Performer by engaging first in the radical innovation activities. Thereafter, it moves from the Radical Performer to the High Performer by diversifying its innovation activities to cover also the incremental improvements.

The requirements for the changes in innovation capacity along with the journey from the Low Performer towards the High Performer are illustrated in Figures 3.3 and 3.4. Figure 3.3 presents the two optional routes for the manufacturing businesses while Figure 3.4 shows the options for the service businesses.

If the Low Performer of the manufacturing businesses takes Route 1 for becoming an Incremental Performer, it should start by improving its exploration and exploitation capabilities (Figure 3.3). In addition, this firm should join the efficiency-related collaborative networks for sharing the costs and it should also improve its abilities to accommodate hidden innovation. Thereafter, if this firm wants to become the High Performer, it should invest even more in the internal RD activities and foster the development of exploration, exploitation and risk management capabilities. In addition, it should join the development-related collaborative networks and search the potential new partners through socializing.

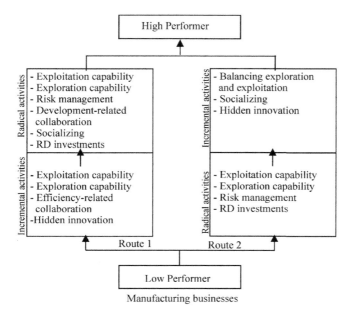

Fig. 3.3. Changes in innovation capacity within the manufacturing businesses.

On the other hand, if the Low Performer of the manufacturing businesses decides to take Route 2 and move first to the Radical Performer, it should allocate more resources in the internal RD activities and focus heavily on enhancing its exploration, exploitation and risk management capabilities. In the case that this firm wants to become the High Performer, after establishing a position as the Radical Performer its resources and capabilities are already close to the required level but it should balance its exploration and exploitation capabilities. In addition, this firm should exploit socializing in order to find new potential partners and improve its abilities to finance hidden innovation.

Correspondingly, within the service businesses the requirements for the changes in innovation capacity differ from those of the manufacturing businesses (see Figure 3.4).

If the Low Performer takes Route 1 for becoming the Incremental Performer, its capabilities and resources are already at the needed level. Nevertheless, it should join the market-related collaborative business

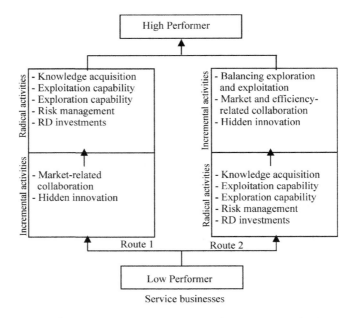

Fig. 3.4.   Changes in innovation capacity within the service businesses.

networks and improve its abilities for hidden innovation. Instead, when this firm wants to continue and become the High Performer, it should allocate a substantial amount of resources in its internal RD activities. In addition, it should make every effort to improve its capabilities.

Finally, if the Low Performer of the service businesses selects Route 2 for becoming the Radical Performer, it should start by allocating heavy investments in the internal RD resources. In addition, it should develop all four types of capabilities. If this firm, after establishing its radical innovation activities, wants to become the High Performer, it should focus on balancing the exploration and exploitation capabilities. In order to strengthen its innovation capacity, this firm should also join the market-related and efficiency-related collaborative networks. Finally, the firm should improve its abilities to accommodate hidden innovation.

In summary, within the manufacturing businesses the journey from the Low Performer to the High Performer starts by allocating resources in capability creation and internal RD activities. Correspondingly, within the service businesses, the similar allocations are needed when a firm engages in radical innovation activities. Instead, the Low Performer seems to possess the required capacity for shifting from the Low Performer to the Incremental Performer.

3.6 Chapter Summary

The aim of this chapter was to explore the capacity of small firms to innovate. This capacity has often been equated with the internal resources allocated to RD activities. Although a strong focus on the RD activities can be an appropriate approach for the technology-intensive larger firms that tend to organize their innovation activities based on the separate projects, it is a less appropriate approach to small firms in which only seldom the innovation activities are separated from other business activities. Instead, innovation takes place in their daily operations, for example in customer collaboration, production activities and quality improvements.

On the other hand, innovation is a collaborative action and also the external resources gained through collaboration are important for enhancing the innovation capacity of small firms.

However, resources alone are not enough. Capabilities are needed to transform the resources to the commercial ends. Hence, while the resources reflect the storage of available materials that are controlled by a firm, the capabilities reflect the abilities of a firm to transform these materials for meeting the innovation goals. Hence, innovation capacity consists of three items: internal resources, capabilities and external resources.

As regards the internal resources allocated to innovation, small firms commonly make low investments in their RD activities. In the sample used in this book, 6 firms out of 10 allocate less than 2% of their annual sales to innovation activities. The most salient finding is, however, that the investments in innovation activities increase while the innovation performer profile shifts from the Low Performer towards the High Performer. The Low and Incremental Performers distinguish from the other profiles based on much lower values allocated in innovation activities. It is natural that the Low Performers do not see any needs for these allocations.

As regards the Incremental Performers, due to the fact that minor improvements will most likely take place integrated in the daily business activities, they do not have a need to separate their innovation activities.

Hence, it can be concluded that the firms with radical innovation activities, that is the High and Radical Performers, have more commonly a need to allocate the above average internal resources for their innovation activities. It is natural because these firms have more sophisticated innovation management practices and for that reason, they may have separated the activities for developing the radical innovations.

However, as mentioned earlier, the internal resources are not enough alone. It is needed to possess the capabilities to integrate, build, and reconfigure these resources. The owner-managers of small firms, who often accumulate their knowledge through learning by doing, play a key role in capability creation. Their individual goals both direct and drive the activities to learn and improve.

Due to the fact that the innovation activities take place integrated in the daily activities of small firms, knowledge and capabilities to innovate will more likely to be improved as a byproduct of these activities. It is natural that the new acquired knowledge is closely related to their current knowledge base. Thus, this knowledge creation dynamics is appropriate for enhancing the existing capacity to innovate resulting in incremental improvements to something that already exists. Instead, if small firms aim to expand to the field that is unrelated to their current knowledge base, they must dedicate their efforts to the regeneration of their existing capabilities and the acquisition of new knowledge. This kind of knowledge creation dynamics is needed for the development of radical innovations.

The empirical results based on the data used in this book demonstrate that the degree of current capabilities increase while the innovation activities in small firms diversify. This supports the arguments presented in prior literature that in small firms the capabilities are created through learning by doing integrated into the innovation activities. Based on the results, especially the activities for developing the radically new innovations demand radical improvements in capabilities while the incremental innovation activities demand only minor improvements in capabilities.

When exploring the capabilities across the innovation performer profiles, it was noticed that the Low and Incremental Performers are better equipped to exploit today's business opportunities while their abilities for exploiting the future opportunities are relatively weak. Although especially the Incremental Performers have realized that they are approaching a competence trap with a risk of becoming incapable of responding to the changes in their business environment. In order to avoid this, they have identified a need for developing their exploration capabilities. This demands substantial efforts dedicated to creating new knowledge with a possibility that they should sacrifice their current profit level. However, these firms do not have the ambitious goals for improving their current low risk management capabilities. For that reason, they may not be ready for such risk taking that would be required.

In regard to the Radical and High Performers, these firms possess a better balance between the exploration and exploitation activities. However, their future goals reveal some differences. Through their balanced goals for exploitation and exploration, the High Performers simultaneously pursue exploiting the current business opportunities as well as exploring the future business opportunities. Instead, the Radical Performers (especially within the manufacturing businesses) tend to favor the exploration capabilities at the expense of exploitation capabilities. Hence, they are capable of creating new innovations while they may be incapable of exploiting commercially these developed innovations. This imbalance could lead to a risk of a failure trap accompanied with a radical but unrewarding change.

It has been commonly argued that innovations cannot be developed in isolation. Especially resource-scarce small firms should collaborate for enhancing their capacity to innovate. In the case that capability creation motivates collaboration, learning may be maximized by collaborating with such partners that have the similar basic knowledge base but the different specialized knowledge base. However, in order to maximize the benefits gained through collaboration, small firms must search for building an optimal structure of partners to support their current and future innovation activities. In this book, the one potential structure was identified by combining the exploration and exploitation activities. Hence, small firms may enhance their capacity for exploiting today's business opportunities as well as tomorrow's business opportunities.

Due to the vital role the owner-managers of small firms play in innovation, also their informal personal networks have a high impact on the activities of their firms. Despite the fact that collaboration may start based on the individual relationships, before long these relationships become a part of the activities of a firm. Thus, socializing represents the source of potential new relationships for small firms.

Prior literature suggests that the balance between the exploitation and exploration activities may be created through the networking activities. Based on the empirical evidence used in this book, the manufacturing businesses have gathered external resources for the development-related and efficiency-related activities while the service businesses have gained benefits for the development-related activities and socializing. Hence, it seems that the manufacturing businesses have been more successful in the balancing task while the service businesses have gained benefits mainly to improve their exploration capabilities.

Another salient finding is that within the manufacturing businesses the networking benefits seem to accumulate while the innovation performer profile shifts from the Low Performer towards the High Performer. Instead, within the service businesses a similar pattern can be located only regarding the market-related activities.

In summary, by combining the theoretical and empirical findings of this chapter, the typical capacity patterns are identified to each four innovation performer profiles. Table 3.4 summarizes these patterns.

As regards *the Low Performers*, they are characterized by a low innovation capacity regarding all four dimensions. In addition, their future goals emphasize developing such a capacity that is appropriate for exploiting today's business opportunities. Thus, these firms tend to continue along their conventional pathways with a risk of facing a competence trap. This may inhibit their abilities to respond to the changing customer needs.

The Incremental Performers differ from the Low Performers by having a somewhat higher degree of capabilities. In addition, they have identified the need for developing such capabilities that will improve their abilities to respond to the future business opportunities. However, taking such a step demands substantial investments in capacity renovation accompanied by a risk of sacrificing their current profit level. The risk management

Table 3.4.   Summary of innovation capacity by innovation performer profiles.

	Low Performer	**Incremental Performer**	**Radical Performer**	**High Performer**
Internal resources	Very low	Low	Above average	High
Abilities to finance hidden innovation	Low	Quite high	Quite low	High
Current capabilities	Low emphasis on exploitation	Low emphasis on exploitation	Very high emphasis on exploitation and exploration	High emphasis on exploitation and exploration
Future capabilities	Emphasis on exploitation	Emphasis on exploitation	Emphasis on exploration	Balanced exploration and exploitation
External resources gained through collaboration	Low	Average	High for exploration	High for exploration and exploitation

capabilities among the Incremental Performers tend to be too low for implementing this kind of strategy.

The Radical Performers are characterized by quite a high innovation capacity. However, their future intentions for capability creation tend to be biased towards the abilities for exploration. There is a risk that the exploration activities drive out the exploitation activities. Hence, the Radical Performers are able to renew their capabilities but simultaneously, due to their inefficient exploitation activities, these firms have a risk of facing a failure trap.

Finally, *the High Performers* are characterized by a high innovation capacity regarding all four dimensions. In addition, their capabilities are in balance for both exploration and exploitation activities. At their best, these two types of capabilities are in a virtuous interaction supporting the firms that simultaneously pursue the exploitation of today's business opportunities as well as the exploration of tomorrow's opportunities.

So, this chapter has described what is the degree and composition of innovation capacity across the different kinds of innovators. Based on the results, the innovation capacity of small firms is associated with their innovation activities suggesting that there exists a two-dimensional process, the innovation activities accelerate capability creation and the capacity to innovate while the new level of innovation capacity accelerates the innovation activities. Especially the activities for developing radical innovations seem to foster capability creation in small firms.

The capacity concept used in this chapter describes the abilities of small firms to innovate as well as their abilities to exploit commercially these innovations. In the best scenario, this should lead to business success in terms of increased sales and improved profits. The question of how the different kinds of innovators have managed to transform their resources into business success will be explored in the next chapter. It focuses on business growth.

References

Amit, R. and Schoemaker, P.J.H. (1993). Strategic assets and organizational rent, *Strategic Management Journal*, 14(1), pp. 33–46.

Barney, J. (1991). Firm resources and sustained competitive advantage, *Journal of Management*, 17(1), pp. 99–120.

Branzei, O. and Vertinsky, I. (2006). Strategic pathways to product innovation capabilities in SMEs, *Journal of Business Venturing*, 21(1), pp. 75–105.

Caloghirou, Y., Kastelli, I. and Tsakanikas, A. (2004). Internal capabilities and external knowledge sources: Complements or substitutes for innovative performance, *Technovation*, 24(1), pp. 29–39.

Caniëls, M.C.J. and Romijn, H.A. (2003). SME clusters, acquisition of technological capabilities and development: Concepts, practice and policy lessons, *Journal of Industry, Competition and Trade*, 3(3), pp. 187–210.

Chan, Y.E., Bhargava, N. and Street, C.T. (2006). Having arrived: The homogeneity of high-growth small firms, *Journal of Small Business Management*, 44(3), pp. 426–440.

Chetty, S. and Agndal, H. (2008). Role of inter-organizational networks and interpersonal networks in an industrial district, *Regional Studies*, 42(2), pp. 175–187.

Cohen, W.M. and Levinthal, D.A. (1990). Absorptive capacity: A new perspective on learning and innovation, *Administrative Science Quarterly*, 35(1), pp. 128–152.

Danneels, E. (2002). The dynamics of product innovation and firm competencies, *Strategic Management Journal*, 23(12), pp. 1095–1121.

Davidsson, P., Steffens, P. and Fitzsimmons, J. (2009). Growing profitable or growing from profits: Putting the horse in front of the cart? *Journal of Business Venturing*, 24(4), pp. 388–406.

de Faria, P., Lima, F. and Santos, R. (2010). Cooperation in innovation activities: The importance of partners, *Research Policy*, 39(8), pp. 1082–1092.

de Jong, J.P.J. and Marsili, O. (2006). The fruit flies of innovations: A taxonomy of innovative small firms, *Research Policy*, 35(2), pp. 213–229.

Dixon, S., Meyer, K. and Day, M. (2014). Building dynamic capabilities of adaptation and innovation: A study of micro-foundations in a transition economy, *Long Range Planning*, 47(4), pp. 186–205.

Eisenhardt, K.M. and Schoonhoven, C.B. (1996). Resource-based view of strategic alliance formation. Strategic and social effects in entrepreneurial firms, *Organization Science*, 7(2), pp. 136–150.

Ettlinger, N. (2003). Cultural economic geography and a relational and microspace approach to trusts, rationalities, networks, and change in collaborative workplaces, *Journal of Economic Geography*, 3(2), pp. 145–171.

Forsman, H. (2008). Business development success in SMEs: A case study approach. *Journal of Small Business and Enterprise Development*, 15(3), pp. 606–622.

Forsman, H. and Rantanen, H. (2011). Small manufacturing and service enterprises as innovators: A comparison by size, *European Journal of Innovation Management*, 14(1), pp. 27–50.

Forsman, H. and Temel, S. (2014). From a non-innovator to a high innovation performer: Networking as a driver. *Regional Studies* (in press).

Forsman, H., Temel, S. and Uotila, M. (2013). Towards sustainable competitiveness: Comparison of the successful and unsuccessful eco-innovators, *International Journal of Innovation Management*, 17(3).

Freel, M.S. and Harrison, R.T. (2006). Innovation and cooperation in the small firm sector: Evidence from Northern Britain, *Regional Studies*, 40(4), pp. 289–305.

Grant, R.M. and Baden-Fuller, C. (2004). A knowledge assessing theory of strategic alliances, *Journal of Management Studies*, 41(1), pp. 61–84.

Gray, C. (2006). Absorptive capacity, knowledge management and innovation in entrepreneurial small firms, *International Journal of Entrepreneurial Behaviour & Research*, 12(6), pp. 345–360.

Hansen, P.A. and Serin, G. (1997). Will low technology products disappear? The hidden innovation processes in low technology industries, *Technological Forecasting and Social Change*, 55 (2), pp. 179–191.

Helfat, C.E. and Peteraf, M.A. (2003). The dynamic resource-based view: Capabilities life cycles, *Strategic Management Journal*, 24(10), pp. 997–1010.

Herrmann, A., Gassmann, O. and Eisert, U. (2007). An empirical study of the antecedents for radical product innovations and capabilities for transformation, *Journal of Engineering and Technology Management*, 24(1–2), pp. 92–120.

Hirsch-Kreinsen, H. (2008). "Low-tech" innovations, *Industry and Innovation*, 15(1), pp. 19–43.

Hurmelinna-Laukkanen, P. and Olander, H. (2014). Coping with rivals' absorptive capacity in innovation activities, *Technovation*, 34(1), pp. 3–11.

Jiang, R.J., Tao, Q.T. and Santoro, M.D. (2010). Alliance portfolio diversity and firm performance, *Strategic Management Journal*, 31(10), pp. 1136–1144.

Jones, O., Macpherson, A. and Thorpe, R. (2010). Learning in owner-managed small firms: Mediating artefacts and strategic space, *Entrepreneurship & Regional Development*, 22(7–8), pp. 649–673.

Kauppila, O.-P. (2010). Creating ambidexterity by integrating and balancing structurally separate interorganizational partnerships, *Strategic Organization*, 8(4), pp. 283–312.

Kirner, E., Kinkel, S. and Jaeger, A. (2009). Innovation paths and the innovation performance of low-technology firms — an empirical analysis of German industry, *Research Policy*, 38(3), pp. 447–458.

Lane, P.J. and Lubatkin, M. (1998). Relative absorptive capacity and interorganizational learning, *Strategic Management Journal*, 19(5), pp. 461–477.

Levine, S. and White, P.E. (1961). Exchange as a conceptual framework for the study of interorganizational relationships, *Administrative Science Quarterly*, 5(4), pp. 583–601.

Lin, C.Y.-Y. and Zhang, J. (2005). Changing structures of SME networks: Lessons from the publishing industry in Taiwan, *Long Range Planning*, 38(2), pp. 145–162.

March, J.G. (1991). Exploration and exploitation in organizational learning, *Organization Science*, 2(1), pp. 71–87.

Mazzarol, T. and Reboud, S. (2008). The role of complementary actors in the development of innovation in small firms, *International Journal of Innovation Management*, 12(2), pp. 223–253.

Nicholas, J., Ledwith, A. and Bessant, J. (2013). Reframing the search space for radical innovation, *Research–Technology Management*, 56(2), pp. 27–35.

Öberg, C. and Grundström, C. (2009). Challenges and opportunities in innovative firms' network development, *International Journal of Innovation Management*, 13(4), pp. 593–613.

Pfeffer, J. and Salancik, G.R. (2003). *The External Control of Organizations*: *A Resource Dependence Perspective*. (Stanford University Press, Stanford, California).

Raisch, S., Birkinshaw, J., Probst, G. and Tushman, M.L. (2009). Organizational ambidexterity: Balancing exploitation and exploration for sustained performance, *Organization Science*, 20(4), pp. 685–695.

Rosenbusch, N., Brinckmann, J. and Bausch, A. (2011). Is innovation always beneficial? A meta-analysis of the relationship between innovation and performance in SMEs, *Journal of Business Venturing*, 26(4), pp. 441–457.

Rowley, T., Behrens, D. and Krackhardt, D. (2000). Redundant governance structures: An analysis of structural and relational embeddedness in the steel and semiconductor industries, *Strategic Management Journal*, 21(3), pp. 369–386.

Shaw, E. (2006). Small firm networking: An insight into contents and motivating factors, *International Small Business Journal*, 24(1), pp. 5–29.

Simon, B.L. (1997). The importance of collaborative know-how. An empirical test of the learning organization, *The Academy of Management Journal*, 40(5), pp. 1150–1174.

Smedlund, A. (2006). The roles of intermediaries in a regional knowledge system, *Journal of Intellectual Capital*, 7(2), pp. 204–220.

Szeto, E. (2000). Innovation capacity: Working towards a mechanism for improving innovation within an inter-organizational network, *The TQM Magazine*, 12(2), pp. 149–158.

Teece, D.J. (2007). Explicating dynamic capabilities: The nature and microfoundations of (sustainable) enterprise performance, *Strategic Management Journal*, 28(13), pp. 1319–1350.

van Gils, A. and Zwart, P.S. (2009). Alliance formation motives in SMEs. An explorative conjoint analysis study, *International Small Business Journal*, 27(1), pp. 5–37.

Williamson, O.E. (1992). Markets hierarchies and the modern corporation, *Journal of Economic Behavior and Organization*, 17(3), pp. 335–352.

Winter, S.G. (2003). Understanding dynamic capabilities, *Strategic Management Journal*, 24(10), pp. 991–995.

Zahra, S.A. and George, G. (2002). Absorptive capacity: A review, reconceptualization, and extension, *Academy of Management Review*, 27(2), pp. 185–203.

Zahra, S.A., Sapienza, H.J. and Davidsson, P. (2006). Entrepreneurship and dynamic capabilities: A review, model and research agenda, *Journal of Management Studies*, 43(4), pp. 917–955.

Zott, C. (2003). Dynamic capabilities and the emergence of intraindustry differential firm performance: Insights from a simulation study, *Strategic Management Journal*, 24(2), pp. 97–125.

Chapter 4

From Innovations to Growth

4.1 Introduction

Growth refers to an expansion in the firm size over a given period of time. The methods to stimulate this expansion in small firms have been of high interest to policy-makers and scholars due to their significant contribution to employment and job creation [Ayyagari et al., 2011; World Bank, 2012]. Despite the increasing number of studies on growth in small businesses, the current literature provides a fragmented body of knowledge for explaining growth in this context.

In their recent article, McKelvie and Wiklund [2010] identified that the studies examining growth can be divided into three approaches: growth as an outcome, the outcome of growth and growth as a process. The first two approaches explore growth as an input or an output by answering the question of why firms are growing. The third approach that have received less attention among scholars and practitioners, examines how firms are growing [cf. Chandler et al., 2009; Achtenhagen et al., 2010]. Dobbs and Hamilton [2007] elaborated these approaches to as many as six different models for exploring growth in small businesses: stochastic, deterministic, descriptive, evolutionary, resource-based and learning-based models.

The stochastic models explain the absence of dominant theory by suggesting that there is a myriad of factors that affect growth (or decline) while the deterministic models try to identify a stable combination of factors relating to individuals, firms and business environments that explain the variation in growth rates. Hence, these two models can answer the questions of why firms are growing and what drives growth [cf. McKelvie and Wiklund, 2010]. Instead, the descriptive models try to understand how firms are growing by identifying the growth process through the sequence of stages or crises without making efforts to explain what drives growth [cf. Churchill and Lewis, 1983]. However, the relevance of these models that present growth as a linear process with predictable stages has been challenged by recent studies [cf. Phelps *et al.*, 2007]. The evolutionary models suggest that growth does not depend on the standard models or the stages of progress. Instead, the nature and timing of growth depends on the interaction of a number of internal and external forces. The resource-based models have a focus on internal resources trying to explain growth through the capabilities and other resources to identify opportunities for growth. Finally, the learning-based models combine the resource-based and evolutionary approaches by trying to understand how and when small business owners can learn and exploit their knowledge most efficiently in order to achieve growth. [Dobbs and Hamilton, 2007.]

This chapter focuses on the question of how the different kinds of innovation performers are growing. It tries to capture the multidimensional phenomenon of growth process with the periods of continuous and temporary changes. On the other hand, by resting on the characteristics of the different kinds of innovators introduced earlier in this book, it tries to find the factors that may be associated with the growth process. Thus, in this chapter the emphasis for explaining growth can be placed into the intersection of the stochastic and descriptive models.

4.2 Innovation as a Source of Growth

It has been commonly argued that the firms that actively aspire to innovation will generate more growth than the non-innovating firms. The main goal of innovation is to transform an idea to a commercial end in a way that it will create value to customers, be superior in competition and generate returns for the innovators [Forsman *et al.*, 2013]. Hence, innovation can be the result of abilities to search, recognize and seize the innovative opportunities while growth can be a result of abilities to commercially exploit the developed innovations [Shane and Venkataraman, 2000]. Further, if growth is profitable, it indicates that a firm has developed an innovation the value of which for its customers is higher than the expenses [Steffens *et al.*, 2009].

However, prior studies present the conflicting empirical findings on innovation and growth reflecting that the relationship between them is not straightforward [OECD, 2002, 2010]. It seems that this relationship is clearer when innovation and growth are examined at a macro level while the results are inconclusive when studying the relationship at a firm level [Tidd, 2001; OECD, 2010].

Although some scholars have identified positive correlation between innovation and growth, others have identified no relationship or even negative correlation between them [Geroski and Machin, 1992; Roper, 1997; Freel, 2000; Rochina-Barrachina *et al.*, 2010; Forsman and Temel, 2011]. Also the direction of effect has remained inconclusive. It has been commonly assumed that innovation affects the growth of a firm. However, the realized growth of a firm in the past may affect its innovation activities. Thus, it remains unclear whether innovation drives growth or realized growth drives innovation [cf. Mason *et al.*, 2009]. On the other hand, innovation may only compensate declining sales from the old products having no effect on the size of firm [OECD, 2010].

Nevertheless, the strategic management literature commonly presents innovations as the sources for competitive advantage that drives growth. Two divergent strategic options, cost efficiency and differentiation, illustrate the dominant logics of a strategy [Porter, 1985; Lechner and Gudmundsson, 2014]. The strategy based on differentiation aims to create more value for customers than competitors. It tries to fulfill the needs of customers in a unique way, hence justifying the higher prices. This strategic option has been linked with the goals for market expansion achieved through the development of product and service innovations. The higher the degree of novelty is, the higher the market-related expectations. On the contrary, the strategy based on cost efficiency aims to reach lower costs than competitors. It often tries to achieve benefits through the economies of scale. This strategic option has been connected with profitability improvements gained through the development of process innovations.

These innovations are often incremental in nature demanding a low level of RD investments. However, the adoption of cost leadership strategy requires substantial financial resources for investing in the fixed assets and changing the production systems.

Previous studies present conflicting recommendations for small firms whether they should adopt a differentiation or cost leadership strategy. OECD [2010] argues that the differentiation strategy aiming at market expansion is riskier than the cost efficiency strategy. Hence, the strategies for market expansion may not be appropriate for the resource-scarce small firms. For that reason they should pursue growth by developing innovations that improve their competitiveness in the existing markets [OECD, 2010]. On the contrary, Lechner and Gudmundsson [2014] present an opposite view. Based on prior literature they have concluded that the differentiation strategy is a potential option for small firms especially in a situation in which competition is based on innovation, speed, flexibility and high quality customer service. Due to the fact that the differentiation strategy requires lower investments, it is more readily accessible for small firms. Instead, cost leadership strategy is less appropriate for small firms due to their resource constraints. [Lechner and Gudmundsson, 2014.] However, Dowling and McGee [1994] point out that the cost leadership strategy could be a potential option for small firms within the industry in which large established companies have dominated for a longer period of time. The late entry allows for flexible small firms the re-engineering of offerings for more efficient production activities.

Nevertheless, Lechner and Gudmundsson [2014] conclude that while the differentiation and cost leadership strategies have opposing logics, they both have a positive impact on firm performance. However, the question of whether a small firm should adopt either one strategic option or a combination has remained unanswered. The positive connection between the purity of strategic option and performance is clearer in larger firms but not in smaller ones [Porter, 1985]. While Lechner and Gudmundsson [2014] recommend a pure option, Dowling and McGee [1994] propose a combination. A small firm may increase its performance by pursuing both strategic options simultaneously. In such a situation, a small firm may take an advantage of innovation in order to use the differentiation strategy as a mean to obtain a low cost position [Dowling and McGee, 1994].

When assessing the strategic options selected by the small firms used in this book, the innovation patterns of four performer profiles suggest that more than 50% of small service businesses and more than 60% of small manufacturing businesses have an exclusive emphasis on their current customers and existing markets. The Low Performers, who have allocated minimal efforts to the innovation activities, rely solely on their existing offerings while the Incremental Performers aim to fulfill the changing needs of their customers by making from time to time minor improvements into their current offerings. The innovation behavior of the Low and Incremental Performers is typical to the firms that have a low level of differentiation in their products and services. In addition, their future goals to continue along with their conventional pathways are not appropriate to the differentiation strategy. While the cost–leadership strategy could be quite an ambitious goal for these firms, they seem to pursue towards cost-efficiency.

On the contrary, the Radical Performers commonly focus on developing new products and services that are new not only to themselves but also to their customers and competitors. Hence, they are targeting for market expansion by relying on radically new product designs. Considering their innovation behavior and ambitious future goals, a differentiation strategy is a potential option for these firms to compete. However, in addition to the new product designs, the successful implementation of differentiation strategy demands high quality in production and delivery, flexibility and speed in customer service as well as excellent after-sales support. Due to the fact that the Radical Performers have low innovation diversity, they may face difficulties in implementing successfully the differentiation strategy. In order to improve their opportunities for success, they should also focus on developing the technical and administrative process innovations.

Finally, the High Performers are firms that have a focus on both their existing customers and the potential new customers acquired through market expansion. They have incorporated a high diversity of innovation activities in their business operations. Their current innovation behavior and the future goals for capability creation reflect that they have a longer term vision to search new business opportunities but they also have their feet in the ground to exploit today's business opportunities. The above richness in characteristics may give a fertile ground for implementing and exploiting a strategy which combines the aspects of both differentiation and cost-efficiency [see also Damanpour *et al.*, 2009; Forsman and Annala, 2011]. At the best, this combination results in the dynamics in which innovation feeds innovation and the output of one innovation will become the input of the next one, thus increasing the opportunities for sales growth through new products and services as well as for reduced expenses through improved processes and procedures [Avermaete *et al.*, 2003; Ambec and Lanoie, 2008; Horbach, 2008].

The above reasoning is also supported by Forsman and Temel [2011], who identified that the firms characterized by the high diversity of innovation activities are among the highest growers. However, they also found that the different kinds of growth indicators may result in different kinds of growth patterns. The question of how growth should be measured in small firms is discussed in the next section.

4.3 Measuring Growth in Small Firms

Delmar *et al.* [2003] argue that prior research has failed to capture the heterogeneous nature of growth for generating cumulative results of firm expansion. They clarify that one reason for this is the fact that firms grow by following several different pathways. Other reasons for the inconclusive findings could be that a variety of different indicators are used to measure growth and a variety of different time frames are used to analyze it [Weinzimmer *et al.*, 1998; Delmar *et al.*, 2003; Achtenhagen *et al.*, 2010].

Thus, the question of which indicators should be used to measure growth is not an easy one to answer. This is an especially challenging question in small businesses in which the quantitative financial figures tend to be infrequently available, if they are available at all. In addition, small firms seem to monitor their success based on such indicators as the feelings of busyness, the chances for survival and the sufficiency of cash for paying the incoming bills [Dess and Robinson, 1984; Jarvis *et al.*, 2000].

In literature, the commonly used indicators for measuring growth are the changes in sales, assets, employment, market share and profits [cf. Delmar *et al.*, 2003; Anyadike-Danes *et al.*, 2009; Achtenhagen *et al.*,

2010]. In the developed economies, growth is often captured by using the market-related and efficiency-related indicators [OECD, 2010]. Due to the fact that in the developing economies it may be difficult to get access to reliable financial data, the change in employment is used to measure growth [Bigsten and Gebreeyesus, 2007; Robson and Obeng, 2008]. Although growth in employment is not a natural goal set by the small business owner-managers, the progress that results in the increased number of employees is of high interest to policy-makers due to the significant role the growing small firms play in job creation [e.g., OECD, 2010; BIS, 2011; Neumark *et al.*, 2011].

As regards the market-related indicators, growth in sales and changes in market share have been widely used indicators for exploring growth [e.g., Delmar *et al.*, 2003; Achtenhagen *et al.*, 2010; McKelvie and Wiklund, 2010]. Nevertheless, market share as an indicator in small firms has been criticized due to the fact that it is difficult to gather such information from these firms. On the other hand, also sales as an indicator have been criticized for not disclosing whether growth is profitable or not. Davidsson *et al.* [2009] warn that growth can even have a negative effect on profitability. They continue that if a firm does not possess resources to implement a strategy towards building hard-to-imitate competitive advantage, sales growth combined with low profits is often only temporary entailing a risk of rapid decline. This easily leads to a situation in which growth must be achieved in fierce head-to-head competition and after a short period of time both the sales growth and profits of these firms will decline below the average [cf. Forsman, 2013].

For that reason, Davidsson *et al.* [2009] recommend that in order to achieve profitable growth, the firms should focus on such growth opportunities that have a good match with their resources. On the other hand, they point out that in the case that the firms underexploit their optimal opportunities to grow, they may gain high profitability based on the non-optimal volume of business. Thus, it is suggested that the market-related indicators should be combined with the efficiency-related indicators such as profitability and productivity [cf. Bonifant *et al.*, 1995; Heunks, 1998; Freel, 2005; Kannebley *et al.*, 2010; Verhees *et al.*, 2010].

While market-related and efficiency-related indicators are justified when measuring growth, it is also needed to recognize the differences between the relative and absolute indicators. The absolute growth indicators measure the value of the annual change while the relative indicators measure the percentage of this change. Weinzimmer *et al.* [1998] point out that the growth indicators can be very sensitive to the firm size leading easily to inconsistent conclusions. For example, the relative indicators may result in high sales growth for small firms while the absolute indicators may result in high growth for large firms [Weinzimmer *et al.*, 1998]. Therefore, it is needed to use a combination of indicators [cf. Achtenhagen *et al.*, 2010]. This is also supported by Delmar *et al.* [2003] who explain that all firms are not growing by proceeding ahead along the same pathways. This is the reason why it is needed to identify the heterogeneous nature of growth process as well as the distinct characteristics of growing firms.

Besides the question of how growth should be measured, also the question of what is an appropriate time frame for measuring growth has been under discussion. If the examination period is too short, it may not allow growth to emerge while if the period is too long, it may be impossible to capture the factors that that drive growth [Storey and Greene, 2010]. The above arguments address criticism towards the growth studies that make use of cross-sectional research designs. These studies may be able to identify the factors that are accompanied with growth but they do not necessarily reveal those factors that contribute to it [Dobbs and Hamilton, 2007]. Hence, such a research setting can identify whether or not innovation is associated with firm growth while it cannot identify the causality between innovation and growth, for example whether innovation drives growth or growth drives innovation.

Also the studies based on the use of only two measurement points have been criticized for three reasons. First, the time frame between these two measurement points is often too short and thus, it is not appropriate for exploring the business dynamics [Tang and Liou, 2010]. Second, growth in small firms does not follow the linear patterns. Instead, it consists of a series of disconnected spurs and jumps to be followed by stable or declining periods [Dobbs and Hamilton, 2007]. Therefore, the studies with only two measurement points cannot explore progress between the start and end points [Weinzimmer *et al.*, 1998; Delmar *et al.*, 2003; Achtenhagen *et al.*, 2010] nor can these studies explore the nature of growth process, for example in terms of regularity and sustainability [Delmar *et al.*, 2003].

Based on the above, it can be concluded that growth should be examined over a longer period of time and by having several measurement points. The OECD [2010] recommends that fast-growth businesses should be studied for a three-year period. However, Tang and Liou [2010] point out that the period of the previous three years is too short a time to account for any business cycle effects. In order to capture also the non-linear changes along with the growth processes, the empirical evidence used in this chapter explores growth during the period of 10 years by having 5 measurement points: 2003–2004, 2005–2006, 2007–2008, 2009–2010 and 2011–2012. The point of 2003–2004 serves as a baseline for measuring growth.

In the following three sections the growth patterns of four innovation performer profiles are identified by using a combination of measures consisting of market-related, efficiency-related and employment-related indicators. The use of multiple indicators is expected to provide a more comprehensive view of growth in small firms. The absolute growth figures by the performer profiles are provided in Appendix, Tables A4.1 and A4.2. In addition, the choice between relative and absolute growth indicators has shown to have a substantial effect on findings. In order to avoid such pitfalls as a result of the sensitivity of indicators, this examination makes use of both absolute and relative indicators to explore growth process across the innovation performer profiles [cf. Weinzimmer *et al.*, 1998; Delmar *et al.*, 2003].

However, Freel [2000] argues that it may be difficult to demonstrate the relationship between growth and innovation when it is explored in heterogeneous groups. He suggests that growth should be studied by using clearer classifications for example by separating the highest growers from the lowest growers. In order to capture more specific characteristics along with the growth process, the patterns regarding the highest and lowest absolute and relative growers are explored. The group of high growers comprises top-100 firms in terms of total growth between 2003 and 2012 while the firms that belong to the weakest 100 firms comprise the group of weak growers. A total of 100 firms correspond to 25.5% of all firms in the sample used in this book.

Finally, also the sustainability and regularity of growth have been largely ignored in growth studies. Delmar *et al.* [2003] add to this that while growth is not static in nature, the prior studies tend to be interested in the occurrence of growth, not on the dynamics of it. However, it is unlikely that gradual monotonous growth and oscillating growth follow the same dynamics [cf. Weinzimmer *et al.*, 1998; Delmar *et al.*, 2003]. On the other hand, it has been recognized that only rarely does high growth tend to persist over time and it seems to turn soon to moderate growth [Daunfeldt and Halvarsson, 2013]. Instead, it has been identified that among small firms there are a number of hidden champions that do not pursue high growth but continuous growth [Lilischkis, 2013].

Based on the above, also the sustainability and regularity of growth process are studied further in the next sections. Three variables are used. The number of growth years demonstrates for how many years out of eight the firms have grown while the number of high growth years indicates how many of them are high growth years during which annual growth is above 25%. Finally, the number of continuous growth years demonstrates the maximum length of a continuous growth period.

4.4 Market-Related Growth in Small Firms

Market-related growth refers to the expansion of a firm in the market through the increasing demand for such products and services that create more value for its customers than the ones offered by its competitors. Due to the fact that small firms more likely will expand in their existing markets, in order to grow they must be capable to sell more to their current customer segments [Oke *et al.*, 2007; OECD, 2010]. Nevertheless, it is not enough. In order to expand into new markets, a small firm must also be capable to attract customers in the new segments.

How the small firms used as a sample in this book have managed to grow in the market will be measured in terms of changes in annual sales. Absolute market-related growth is measured by the changes in the value of annual sales while relative market-related growth is measured by the ratio of change in annual sales. The basis for calculating the relative change in annual sales is the mean value of the years 2003–2004.

Figure 4.1 illustrates how the small manufacturing businesses have grown along with the period of 10 years from 2003 to 2012.

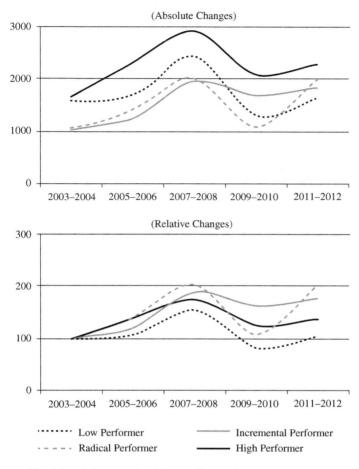

Fig. 4.1.   Sales growth of the small manufacturing businesses.

When looking at the absolute sales values, the data used in this book demonstrates that all performer profiles experienced a positive progress during the favorable economic situation between 2003 and 2008. In 2009, the world encountered a deep recession which resulted in a dramatic drop in sales. In 2009–2010, sales declined by 30% to 50% within three out of the four innovation performer profiles. Nevertheless, the drop was temporary and sales started to grow again in 2011. However, one exception emerges from the data. The Incremental Performers have a divergent trend. While they experienced a smooth growth in absolute sales values during the upswing, these firms suffered only a hardly noticeable small decline in sales during the downturn.

The absolute sales values also reveal that at the beginning of the examination period the extent of business within the Low and High Performers was larger than within the Incremental and Radical Performers. However, at the end of the examination period the difference is narrower. The Incremental and Radical Performers grew faster and by the end of examination period they overtook the Low Performers in terms of absolute sales.

The relative changes in annual sales demonstrate similar growth patterns as the absolute changes (see the bottom part of Figure 4.1). During the favorable economic situation all profiles had a growing trend that turned into decline during the recession. The Radical Performers suffered from the most dramatic decline during the recession. The Low Performers experienced only slight relative growth during the upswing but during the downturn they were confronted with almost as dramatic a drop as the Radical Performers. The relative changes within the Incremental and High Performers are smoother. However, at the end of the examination period the innovating firms have started to recover from the recession and turn back to the growing direction. The speediest recovery is located within the Radical Performers. Instead, the Low Performers have hardly been able to catch up the level they had in 2003–2004.

Growth among the service businesses share several similarities with the manufacturing businesses. As can be noticed from Figure 4.2, the innovating firms, that is the Incremental, Radical and High Performers, have been in the promising growth direction during the favorable economic situation while absolute sales within the Low Performers have remained quite stable. The most striking graph is located within the High Performers. They doubled their absolute sales during a relatively short but rapid growth period between 2005 and 2008. However, during the economic downturn these firms started a smooth decline. Finally, the Radical Performers had the highest annual absolute sales level at the beginning of the examination period while at the end of the period, the Incremental and High Performers have grown faster and achieved almost the same absolute level.

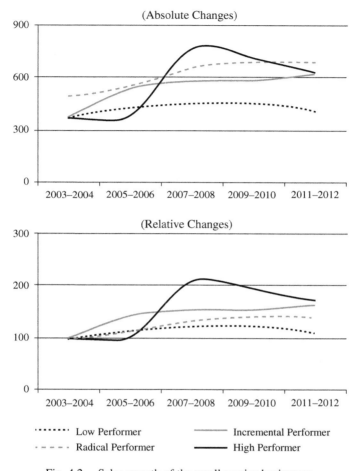

Fig. 4.2.   Sales growth of the small service businesses.

What comes to relative market-related growth within the service businesses, the bottom part of Figure 4.2 demonstrates that fluctuation within the service businesses have been lower than within the manufacturing businesses. The High and Incremental Performers have been the fastest growers while the Radical and Low Performers have more stable growth curves. The High Performers have a distinguishable curve. Despite the smooth decline since 2009, their high growth period between 2005 and

2008 shifted them above all other profiles in terms of relative market-related growth.

It can be summarized that during the period of 10 years, the High Performers of the manufacturing businesses experienced the highest growth in terms of absolute changes while the Incremental and Radical Performers experienced the highest growth in terms of relative changes in annual sales. Instead, within the service businesses the High and Incremental Performers had the highest growth. Within both sectors the slowest growth was identified within the Low Performers.

Hence, the above results indicate that innovating small firms outperform the non-innovating firms in terms of market-related success. On the other hand, Lotti *et al.* [2009] argue that the smallest firms try to grow to a minimum size that allows them to run their businesses efficiently. The growth process of the Incremental Performers within the manufacturing businesses as well as that of the High Performers within the service businesses could reflect that these quite small firms have taken a growth sprint in order to achieve the needed size to efficiently operate in their market.

When exploring the growth processes, it was also noticed that the small manufacturing businesses tend to have more fluctuation in their sales than the small service businesses. During the upswing they experienced rapid growth while during the recession they were confronted with a dramatic drop. Instead, within the service businesses, firms experienced smoother growth during the upswing but it turned into a stable or smoothly declining progress during the downturn. However, the High Performers within the service businesses are exceptions. Their growth curve is characterized by higher fluctuation.

The growth processes are also examined by identifying the highest and weakest growers across the performer profiles. In addition, the sustainability and regularity of growth processes are explored. Table 4.1 presents the summary of these aspects for the market-related growth process.

As regards the highest and weakest growers, it can be noticed that the absolute and relative indicators lead to divergent findings. More than one-third of the manufacturing businesses belong to the highest absolute growers while only one-fourth of them belong to the highest relative growers. Correspondingly, when one-fourth of the service businesses belong to the highest relative growers, only one out of six firms belongs to the highest absolute growers.

Table 4.1. Characteristics of the market-related growth process.

Manufacturing businesses	Low Performer	Incremental Performer	Radical Performer	High Performer	Total
Share of highest and weakest growers					
Share of high absolute growers	25.0	30.0	37.9	45.7	34.0
Share of high relative growers	25.0	23.3	34.5	26.1	25.9
Share of weak absolute growers	43.8	23.3	27.6	21.7	26.9
Share of weak relative growers	37.5	21.1	17.2	19.6	22.8
Sustainability and regularity					
No. of growth years	5.0	5.2	5.4	5.2	5.2
No. of high growth years	1.7	2.2	2.1	2.0	2.0
No. of continuous growth years	3.2	3.3	3.5	3.2	3.3

Service businesses	Low Performer	Incremental Performer	Radical Performer	High Performer	Total
Share of highest and weakest growers					
Share of high absolute growers	3.4	16.4	11.8	27.1	16.9
Share of high relative growers	13.8	24.7	17.6	35.6	25.1
Share of weak absolute growers	27.6	21.9	26.5	23.7	24.1
Share of weak relative growers	27.6	30.1	32.4	23.7	28.2
Sustainability and regularity					
No. of growth years	5.1	5.1	4.9	5.5	5.2
No. of high growth years	0.9	1.5	1.4	2.1	1.6
No. of continuous growth years	3.4	3.4	3.0	4.0	3.5

When looking at the differences across the innovation performer profiles, it can be observed that the use of relative and absolute indicators, even within these firms with fewer than 50 employees, leads to slightly different conclusions [cf. Delmar *et al.*, 2003]. Within the manufacturing firms the highest absolute growers are located among the High Performers while the highest relative growers are found among the Radical Performers. Instead, within the service businesses, the High Performers accommodate the highest proportion of both the absolute and relative growers.

Regarding the weakest growth, among the manufacturing firms, the high proportion of the weakest growers are located within the Low Performers while among the service businesses the Low Performers accommodate the highest proportion of weak growers in terms of absolute growth while the Radical Performers include the highest share of weak performers in terms of relative growth.

Despite the differences between the absolute and relative indicators, a salient finding is that high market-related growth more likely emerges among the High Performers while weak growth emerges among the Low Performers. However, regarding relative high growth and relative weak growth, there exists some variation across the innovation performer profiles.

In addition to high growth also the regularity and sustainability of growth has started to receive more attention among scholars, practitioners and policy-makers. As Table 4.1 shows, the number of growth years is above five indicating that on average the small firms of this sample have grown during five out of eight years between 2005 and 2012. Within the manufacturing businesses, two of these years have been high growth years while within the service businesses the number of high growth years is lower. The number of continuous growth years varies between three and four.

In summary, Weinzimmer *et al.* [1998] warn that the absolute and relative indicators can lead to conflicting conclusions. The results of this examination demonstrate that when used to measure market-related growth within the group of small firms, the absolute indicators may favor the manufacturing businesses that are larger in size. Correspondingly, the relative indicators may favor the smaller service businesses. The use of these indicators results in slightly different conclusions especially regarding high growth. Hence, it is justified to use both types of indicators to measure growth in the context of small business. In addition, it is needed to use them both in order to capture the nature of the growth process.

It can be concluded that the High Performers perform quite well in terms of market-related growth while the Low Performers mostly underperform compared with the other profiles. The Incremental and Radical Performers are between these two profiles. Thus, it can be suggested that the relationship between market-related growth and the diversity of innovation activities is stronger than the relationship between growth and the type of innovation activities.

On the other hand, neither of the above indicators reveals whether growth is profitable or not. While it is a common assumption that market-related expansion is positively associated with profitability, Davidsson *et al.* [2009] warn that growth in sales does not automatically lead to increased profits. Instead, the firms with low profits are not the most promising ones to achieve high profitability as a result of their market expansion. The issue how the different innovation performer profiles have managed to grow in terms of profits is explored in the next section.

4.5 Efficiency-Related Growth in Small Firms

Efficiency-related growth refers to the performance of a firm to create value and appropriate financial returns. Hence, profitability is the essence of value creation and appropriation. For that reason, the common indicators used to measure this type of growth are profits and profit ratios. While growing profitability has commonly been connected with the adoption of cost efficiency strategy [York, 2009; Verhees *et al.*, 2010], there are, however, two main ways to grow in terms of profits. First, by lowering the costs through efficient systems and processes, and second, by increasing the price level through differentiation. Davidsson *et al.* [2009] point out that in order to achieve profitable growth a firm should exploit such opportunities that have a good match with its resources. This means that the goals for growth should be in balance with the resources of a firm.

The question of how small firms have managed to balance their resources with goals in order to achieve efficiency-related growth is examined in this section. Absolute efficiency-related growth is measured by the changes in the value of annual operating profits and the relative growth is measured by using the ratio of change in operating profits. The baseline for calculating the relative change is the mean value of the years 2003–2004.

Figure 4.3 presents how the four innovation performer profiles within the manufacturing businesses have grown during the period of 10 years.

As can be noticed, between the years 2003 and 2008, efficiency-related growth in terms of absolute operating profits was the highest among the High and Incremental Performers while the Radical Performers experienced only a slightly positive trend. Instead, the Low Performers had a fluctuating process.

Affected by the recession, all four profiles started to decline in 2009 but the High and Incremental Performers encountered a dramatic drop in

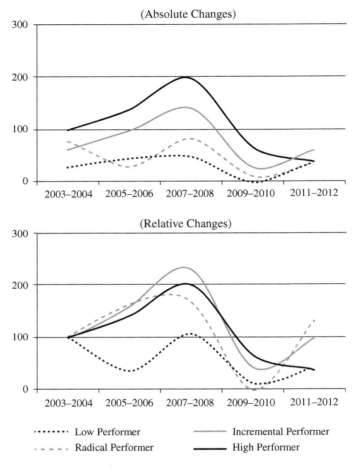

Fig. 4.3.   Growth in operating profits of the manufacturing businesses.

their operating profits. Despite the fact that in 2011 all profiles started a slow recovery, at the end of the examination period three out of four profiles were still below the absolute profit level they had at the beginning of the examination period (in 2003–2004). The Radical Performers are the exceptions. They have managed to bypass the level they possessed 10 years ago.

The above patterns change slightly when efficiency-related growth is explored in terms of the relative changes in operating profits. The bottom part of Figure 4.3 illustrates that the Incremental, Radical and High Performers experienced very high growth during the favorable economic situation while they also encountered a dramatic drop during the downturn. Instead, the Low Performers had a fluctuating process with jumps and drops. In 2011, all performer profiles started to recover. When measured by the relative changes in operating profits, the Radical Performers got the best start for the recovery and they bypassed the starting level they had in 2003–2004.

Regarding the service businesses, the High and Low Performers experienced the highest absolute growth during the upswing in 2003–2008 while in 2009–2010 this promising growth turned into a steady decline (Figure 4.4). Instead, the Incremental and Radical performers had quite a moderate growth progress during the favorable economic situation which turned into decline during the recession. In 2011, the Radical Performers started a quick recovery while the other three profiles still had a declining or stable trend.

The bottom part of Figure 4.4 demonstrates that the relative changes within the service businesses are smoother than those within the manufacturing businesses. The High Performers are exceptions. They distinguish from other profiles based on their very high growth. However, during the recession it turned into a dramatic decline. The Radical Performers stand out based on their quick recovery from recession at the end of the examination period. Finally, the Low and Incremental Performers have quite similar curves characterized by low fluctuation. During the upswing they started with quite a stable progress which turned into smooth decline during the recession.

When looking at the groups of high and weak growers, it can be noticed from Table 4.2 that the High Performers have a high proportion of the highest growers. In addition, also the Radical Performers of the manufacturing businesses accommodate a high proportion of high growers. An interesting finding is that these same profiles accommodate also a high number of weak growers. It reflects that efficiency-related growth is fluctuating more strongly within these two profiles. Instead, the Incremental and Low Performers are characterized by a more stable progress.

Regarding the regularity and sustainability of the efficiency-related growth process, the average number of growth years is approximately

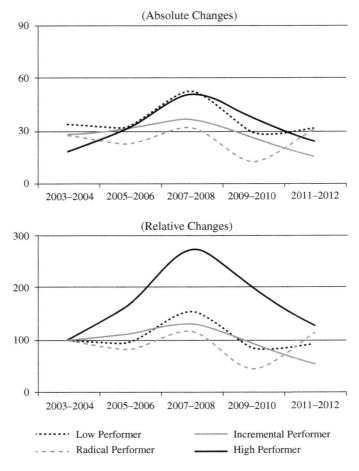

Fig. 4.4.   Growth in operating profits of the service businesses.

three and above two of them are high growth years. The patterns within the manufacturing businesses are quite similar across the profiles but within the service businesses there exists some variation. Somewhat surprisingly the Radical Performers have the lowest number of growth years as well as high growth years while the Low Performers have the highest values for both indicators. Finally, the number of continuous growth years is below two. Also regarding this indicator, there exists variation within

Table 4.2.   Characteristics of the efficiency-related growth process.

Manufacturing businesses	Low Performer	Incremental Performer	Radical Performer	High Performer	Total
Share of highest and weakest growers					
High absolute growers	18.8	28.9	34.5	30.4	28.4
High relative growers	21.9	22.2	37.9	37.0	27.9
Weak absolute growers	34.4	31.1	34.5	34.8	33.0
Weak relative growers	18.8	25.6	27.6	30.4	25.9
Sustainability and regularity					
No. of growth years	2.7	3.0	2.8	2.8	2.9
No. of high growth years	2.3	2.3	2.1	2.2	2.2
No. of continuous growth years	1.3	1.3	1.4	1.4	1.3

Service businesses	Low Performer	Incremental Performer	Radical Performer	High Performer	Total
Share of highest and weakest growers					
High absolute growers	24.1	21.9	17.6	25.4	22.6
High relative growers	17.2	24.7	11.8	30.5	23.1
Weak absolute growers	13.8	15.1	14.7	25.4	17.9
Weak relative growers	24.1	24.7	29.4	23.7	25.1
Sustainability and regularity					
No. of growth years	3.4	3.3	2.5	3.2	3.1
No. of high growth years	2.5	2.4	1.7	2.4	2.3
No. of continuous growth years	1.7	1.2	1.2	1.5	1.4

the service businesses. The Low Performers possess the longest continuous growth period while the Radical Performers have the shortest one.

In summary, when comparing the efficiency-related growth curves between the service and manufacturing businesses, it can be noticed that the service businesses have smoother absolute profit levels but they also have much lower fluctuation during the economic turning points. Within both sectors, the High Performers have experienced the most promising growth during the favorable economic situation while they also have experienced the most dramatic drop during the economic downturn. The Radical Performers are characterized by fluctuation in terms of relative changes in efficiency-related growth but they have started the most promising recovery after the recession.

As regards the regularity of growth, the results indicate that across the innovation performer profiles there exists more variation within the service businesses while the patterns within the manufacturing businesses are quite similar. Finally, it has been more challenging for small firms to achieve regularity and sustainability in efficiency-related growth than in market-related growth. The number of growth years and the number of continuous growth years are much lower for profits than they are for annual sales.

4.6 Employment-Related Growth in Small Firms

There are several reasons why growth in employment should be included as one approach to the studies having focus on small businesses. While the expansion in employment is not a goal for the owner-managers of small firms, it is of high interest to policy-makers. On the other hand, expansion in employment could start the growth process within the small firms that have launched new business activities. In addition, the employment patterns in small firms are not as sensitive to economic fluctuation as the market-related growth patterns [Delmar *et al.*, 2003; Forsman and Temel, 2011]. Due to the fact that the number of employees reported by small firms often does not make a distinction whether the employees are part or full-time, in this examination paid salaries are used as an indicator to reflect growth in employment. Thus, it is assumed that the changes in paid salaries correspond to the changes in the number of employees.

Figure 4.5 presents the patterns of employment-related growth within the manufacturing businesses.

When looking at the trend of paid absolute salaries within the small manufacturing businesses, it can be observed that during the period of 10 years, the High and Radical Performers experienced the most promising growth while within the Low and Incremental Performers growth patterns are progressing more steadily. Affected by the recession in 2009, within the Radical Performers the paid absolute salaries dropped while there are only minor changes within the other performer profiles. The bottom part of Figure 4.5 illustrates that the relative changes in paid salaries are quite similar to the absolute changes.

Regarding the progress of paid salaries within the service businesses (see Figure 4.6), it can be noticed that the highest absolute growth is located among the High Performers followed by the Incremental

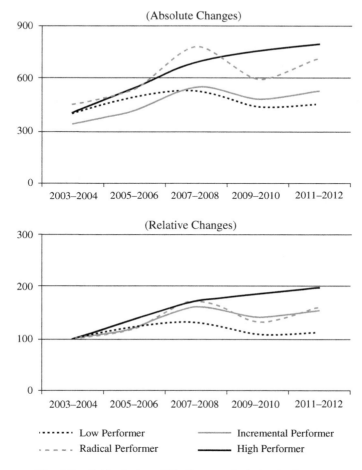

Fig. 4.5.   Paid salaries within the manufacturing businesses.

Performers. Instead, within the Low and Radical Performers growth progressed more steadily. However, this growth was temporary and the paid salaries started to decline between 2007 and 2009.

The progress regarding the relative changes in paid salaries (the bottom part of Figure 4.6) illustrates similar growth patterns to the absolute changes. However, the differences across the performer profiles are larger. During the period of 10 years, the Incremental and High Performers had

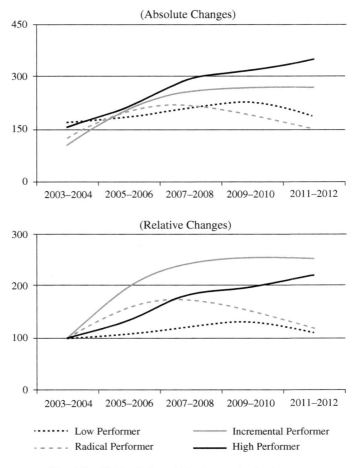

Fig. 4.6. Paid salaries within the service businesses.

steady growth in paid salaries while the Low and Radical Performers started with slow growth that turned into a declining trend.

Considering the dramatic drop in market-related and efficiency-related indicators during the recession, the growth patterns in Figure 4.6 suggest that within the service businesses the High and Incremental Performers could afford to keep their employees even in the conditions of declining business performance.

Hence, it can be summarized that economic turning points have not affected as heavily the paid salaries as they seem to have affected the market-related and efficiency-related growth patterns. During the favorable economic situation the paid salaries are growing while during the downturn the majority of small firms try to keep their employees even in the conditions of declining sales and profits [cf. Forsman and Temel, 2011]. However, especially the Radical Performers may have some tendency to consider their employees as a flexible resource to respond to the economic turning points.

In regard to the highest growers, the results in Table 4.3 indicate once again that the absolute indicators return higher values to the manufacturing businesses while the relative indicators favor the smaller service businesses. Instead, the differences regarding the weakest growers are not as straightforward.

When looking at the differences across the performers profiles, it can be noticed that within both sectors the High Performers have a large proportion of high absolute and relative growers while the Low Performers have a high share of weak growers (Table 4.3). In addition, within the service businesses also the Radical Performers accommodate a high number of weak growers.

Regarding the regularity and sustainability of the growth process, the patterns are quite similar between the service and manufacturing businesses. Within both sectors the average number of the growing years is four-and-a-half, and below two of them are identified to be high growth years. The length of continuous growth period is approximately three years.

While within the manufacturing businesses there are only minor differences in regularity across the performer profiles, within the service businesses there exists more variation. The regularity and sustainability of growth are the lowest within the Radical Performers. In addition, the Low Performers are characterized by a low number of high growth years.

It can be concluded that within both the manufacturing and service businesses the High Performers have experienced the most promising growth process during the favorable economic situation. During the downturn they still have maintained moderate growth. Within both sectors also the growth patterns of the Low Performers are quite similar being

Table 4.3.   Characteristics of the employment-related growth process.

Manufacturing businesses	Low Performer	Incremental Performer	Radical Performer	High Performer	Total
Share of highest and weakest growers					
High absolute growers	21.9	26.7	31.0	39.1	29.4
High relative growers	15.6	24.4	20.7	28.3	23.4
Weak absolute growers	37.5	30.0	24.1	21.7	28.4
Weak relative growers	43.8	32.2	17.2	28.3	31.0
Sustainability and regularity					
No. of growth years	4.3	4.4	4.6	4.6	4.5
No. of high growth years	1.0	1.3	1.6	1.3	1.3
No. of continuous growth years	2.8	2.9	3.1	3.1	3.0

Service businesses	Low Performer	Incremental Performer	Radical Performer	High Performer	Total
Share of highest and weakest growers					
High absolute growers	—	23.3	17.6	32.2	21.5
High relative growers	6.9	27.4	29.4	37.3	27.7
Weak absolute growers	27.6	20.5	29.4	18.6	22.6
Weak relative growers	27.6	21.3	26.5	10.2	20.0
Sustainability and regularity					
No. of growth years	4.1	4.8	3.9	4.7	4.5
No. of high growth years	0.8	1.4	1.2	1.9	1.4
No. of continuous growth years	2.8	3.3	2.7	3.4	3.1

characterized by a stable or slow growth process during the upswing while it has turned into a smooth decline during the recession.

Instead, there are differences between the Radical and Incremental Performers. While the Radical Performers within the manufacturing businesses are characterized by fluctuating growth in paid salaries, within the service businesses they are characterized by moderate but steady growth during the upswing turning into moderate decline during the recession. Correspondingly, while the Incremental Performers within the manufacturing businesses are characterized by a slightly growing trend, within the service businesses they have experienced high growth in paid salaries during the favorable economic situation and during the downturn they have maintained the achieved level.

Finally, when comparing the process of employment-related growth with market-related and efficiency-related growth, it can be observed that small firms may indeed have a tendency to avoid strong fluctuation in terms of the number of employees (and the paid salaries).

4.7 Chapter Summary

While innovation reflects the outcome of abilities to search, recognize and seize the innovative opportunities, growth reflects the outcome of abilities to commercially exploit these innovations. The latter outcome, business growth, was in the center point of this chapter. The main question to direct the examination was: How are the different kinds of innovation performers growing?

Although it has commonly been assumed that innovation drives growth, prior studies provide more or less inconclusive results regarding this relationship. While some studies have identified positive correlation between innovation and growth, others have identified no relationship or even negative correlation between them. Also the direction of influence has remained unclear. Innovation may drive growth or past growth may drive innovation. On the other hand, while innovation may increase sales from the new products, at the same time sales from the old products may decline. In such a case innovation only helps a firm maintain its current size.

In order to explain the inconclusive results, prior studies provide a variety of reasons, such as the heterogeneous nature of growth pathways among small firms, the differences in indicators for measuring growth, the number of measurement points and the length of examination period. Prior literature also criticizes that all too often growth is studied as a linear progress based on two measurement points by using the single indicators for measuring growth during a short period of time.

Given the above criticism, this chapter took another approach to explore growth. Instead of studying the relationship between innovation and growth, it focused on exploring the growth process within the different kinds of innovators. In order to capture the nature of this process, the length of examination period is as long as 10 years having 5 measurement points.

The question of which indicators should be used to measure growth in small firms is not an easy one to answer. The quantitative financial indicators are commonly suggested by the scholars while the owner-managers of small firms tend to monitor their success by using such indicators as the feelings of busyness, the chances for survival and the sufficiency of cash for paying the incoming bills. Due to their unsophisticated performance measurement systems and practices, financial information tends to be available only once a year when small firms must submit their annual accounts for the official purposes. The empirical evidence of this chapter makes use of this official data comprising the annual accounts. It includes information for exploring market-related, efficiency-related and employment-related growth.

It has been recognized that there are differences in growth patterns when measured by the absolute and relative indicators. The absolute growth indicators measure the value of the annual change while the relative indicators measure the percentage of this change. These indicators can be very sensitive to the firm size leading easily to erratic conclusions. The relative indicators tend to result in high growth for small firms while the absolute indicators tend to result in high growth for large firms. For that reason, both relative and absolute indicators were used concurrently in this chapter.

Based on the empirical evidence used in this chapter, the most salient finding is that the innovating small firms outperform the non-innovating ones in all three growth dimensions. The Low Performers that represent the non-innovators and the firms characterized by very poor innovation activities are below average regarding market-related, efficiency-related and employment-related growth. Correspondingly, the High Performers that represent the firms characterized by diversified innovation activities have experienced high market-related, efficiency-related and employment-related growth. Instead, the results are not as conclusive among the Incremental and Radical Performers. Differences emerge between the growth dimensions as well as between the results of relative and absolute indicators.

In general, the absolute indicators seem to favor the manufacturing businesses that are larger in size while the relative indicators result in higher growth to the smaller service businesses. For that reason the main findings have been summarized separately for the manufacturing and service businesses. Table 4.4 presents the main characteristics of growth process for the manufacturing businesses while Table 4.5 shows those for the service businesses.

Table 4.4.   Summary of growth process within the manufacturing firms.

	Low Performer	**Incremental Performer**	**Radical Performer**	**High Performer**
Strategic option	Defending	Cost-efficiency	Differentiation	Cost-efficiency & differentiation
Average growth in 2003–2012				
Market-related	Very low	High (relative)	High (relative)	High (absolute)
Efficiency-related	Very low	High	Average	Quite High
Employment-related	Low	Below average	Above average	High
Growth process[a]				
High growers			(MA, EF)	(MA, EF, EM)
Weak growers	(MA, EM)		(EF)	(EF)

Note: [a](MA) = market-related, (EF) = efficiency-related and (EM) = employment-related.

Both scholars and policy-makers have been especially interested in high-growth firms. Based on the empirical evidence used in this book, it can be concluded that within the manufacturing businesses high market-related growth will more likely take place within the Radical and High Performers, high efficiency-related growth within the Incremental and High Performers and high employment-related growth within the High Performers. Instead, the Low Performers have a weak growth progress regarding all three growth dimensions.

Regarding the nature of growth processes of the manufacturing businesses, it was noticed that the Radical and High Performers are the most vulnerable to recession. Instead, the Low Performers have suffered only from declining sales while the Incremental Performers have suffered from declining profits.

In regard to the service businesses, Table 4.5 summarizes the main characteristics of their growth processes.

Within the service businesses, the High Performers have experienced high growth in terms of all three growth dimensions while the Low and Radical Performers belong to those that have experienced low growth or declining progress. Instead, within the Incremental Performers the progress varies between the different growth dimensions. While their market-related growth is average and efficiency-related growth is quite low, they have much higher values in terms of employment-related growth.

Table 4.5.   Summary of growth process within the service firms.

	Low Performer	Incremental Performer	Radical Performer	High Performer
Typical strategic option	Defending	Cost-efficiency	Differentiation	Cost-efficiency & differentiation
Average growth in 2003–2012				
Market-related	Very low	Average	Quite low	High
Efficiency-related	Below average	Quite low	Very low	High
Employment-related	Very low	Very high	Low	High
Nature of growth process[a]				
High growers				(MA, EF, EM)
Weak growers	(MA, EM)		(MA, EF, EM)	(EF)

Note: [a](MA) = market-related, (EF) = efficiency-related and (EM) = employment-related.

When searching the high-growth firms within the service businesses, it was noticed that the High Performers accommodate the highest share of these firms that belong to the top quarter in terms of growth. Correspondingly, the majority of weak growers are located among the Low and Radical Performers. Somewhat surprisingly, also the High Performers accommodate a high number of the weakest growers in terms of efficiency-related growth.

In regard to the regularity and sustainability of growth, the empirical evidence indicates the highest values within the High Performers while the values are the lowest among the Low and Radical Performers.

Based on the above, it is easy to conclude that the firms that actively pursue innovation will generate more growth than the non-innovating firms. On the other hand, it is just as easy to conclude that growth in small firms follows several different pathways [Delmar *et al.*, 2003]. The results presented in this chapter reveal a rich diversity of growth patterns across the different kinds of innovators.

Nevertheless, some strong characteristics were identified. For example, if one wants to find the market-related growers, they will more likely to be located within the High and Radical Performers. Instead, if the efficiency-related growers should be located, it would be better to search them within the Incremental and High Performers. Those who want to find the employment-related growers should start from the

Incremental and High Performers. Finally, if one wants to locate the firms that are growing in terms of all three dimensions, market-related, efficiency-related and employment-related growth, he should search them within the High Performers. Correspondingly, the firms that possess a declining trend in all dimensions are more likely found among the Low Performers.

The strategic management literature has discussed whether small firms should adopt differentiation or cost-efficiency strategy. While some scholars have recognized that the differentiation strategy is more successful in the context of small business, others have identified that they more likely will be successful by adopting the cost-efficiency strategy. On the other hand, some scholars have suggested that in order to be successful, it is needed to implement both types of strategies.

The characteristics of innovation performer profiles reflect their strategic preferences. When looking at this issue based on the empirical evidence offered in this book, it can be concluded that the Radical Performers that more likely have adopted a pure differentiation strategy, have achieved high market-related growth within the manufacturing businesses while within the service businesses these firms have failed to grow. The relatively low degree of efficiency-related strengths indicates that these firms have not been able to organize their internal processes for achieving high quality in production, delivery and customer service. Hence, without the efforts to increase their internal efficiency, these small firms are not able to build long-term competitiveness.

Correspondingly, the Incremental Performers that represent the firms that have more likely adopted a pure cost-efficiency strategy, have achieved high efficiency-related and market-related growth within the manufacturing businesses while they have achieved high employment-related growth within the service businesses. These firms have efficient internal processes that enable them to achieve quite a high profit level. However, due to their reactive innovation behavior and minimal efforts given to the innovation activities, there is a risk of losing their competitiveness in the future.

The High Performers that represent the firms that have adopted a combination of differentiation and cost-efficiency strategies have achieved high growth in terms of all dimensions. These firms have balanced their exploration and exploitation activities. They focus on fulfilling the expressed needs of their current customers as well as exploring the unexpressed needs of the potential future customers. Their diversified innovation activities and proactive innovative behavior may enable them to maintain their competitive trend.

Finally, the Low Performers that seem to have adopted a defending strategy are in a survival battle. Their progress has a stable or declining trend regarding all three growth dimensions.

While the characteristics of each innovation performer profile reflect the competitiveness of firm, there is, however, a need to explore how the different kinds of growers have achieved their competitiveness. This issue will be discussed in the next chapter. It focuses on competitiveness in small firms and more precisely on it how superior competitiveness can be achieved and how it can be lost.

References

Achtenhagen, L., Naldi, L. and Melin, L. (2010). "Business growth" — Do practitioners and scholars really talk about the same thing? *Entrepreneurship, Theory and Practice*, 34(2), pp. 289–316.

Ambec, S. and Lanoie, P. (2008). Does it pay to be green? A systematic overview, *Academy of Management Perspectives*, 22(4), pp. 45–62.

Anyadike-Danes, M., Bonner, K., Hart, M. and Mason, C. (2009). *Measuring Business Growth: High-growth firms and their contribution to employment in the UK*. Research Report. (NESTA, London). Online. Available at: http://www.nesta.org.uk/sites/default/files/measuring_business_growth.pdf (Accessed 15.12.2013).

Avermaete, T., Viaene, J., Morgan, E.J. and Crawford, N. (2003). Determinants of innovation in small food firms, *European Journal of Innovation Management*, 6(1), pp. 8–17.

Ayyagari, M., Demirgüc-Kunt, A. and Maksimovic, V. (2011). *Small vs. Young Firms Across the World. Contribution to Employment, Job Creation and Growth*. Policy Research Working Paper 5631, (The World Bank, Development Research Group, Finance and Private Sector Development Team). Online. Available at: http://elibrary.worldbank.org/doi/pdf/10.1596/1813-9450-5631 (Accessed 15.12.2013).

Bigsten, A. and Gebreeyesus, M. (2007). The small, the young, and the productive: Determinants of manufacturing firm growth in Ethiopia, *Economic Development and Cultural Change*, 55(4), pp. 813–840.

BIS (2011). *Innovation and Research Strategy for Growth*. Department for Business, Innovation and Skills. (BIS, London). Online. Available at: https://www.gov.uk/government/publications/innovation-and-research-strategy-for-growth (Accessed 02.09.2013).

Bonifant, B.C., Arnold, M.B. and Long, F.J. (1995). Gaining competitive advantage through environmental investments, *Business Horizons*, 38(4), pp. 37–47.

Chandler, G.N., McKelvie, A. and Davidsson, P. (2009). Asset specificity and behavioral uncertainty as moderators of the sales growth — employment growth relationship in emerging ventures, *Journal of Business Venturing*, 24(4), pp. 373–387.

Churchill, N.C. and Lewis, V.L. (1983). The five stages of small business growth, *Harvard Business Review*, 61(3), pp. 30–50.

Damanpour, F., Walker, R.M. and Avellaneda, C.N. (2009). Combinative effects of innovation types and organizational performance: A longitudinal study of service organizations, *Journal of Management Studies*, 46(4), pp. 650–675.

Daunfeldt, S.-O. and Halvarsson, D. (2013). *Are high-growth firms one-hit wonders? Evidence from Sweden*, Working Paper, (KTH, Economics, Stockholm). Online. Available at: http://kth.diva-portal.org/smash/get/diva2:605656/FULLTEXT01.pdf (Accessed 08.11.2013).

Davidsson, P., Steffens, P. and Fitzsimmons, J. (2009). Growing profitable or growing from profits: Putting the horse in front of the cart? *Journal of Business Venturing*, 24(4), pp. 388–406.

Delmar, F., Davidsson, P. and Gartner, W.B. (2003). Arriving at high-growth firm, *Journal of Business Venturing*, 18(2), pp.189–216.

Dess, G.G. and Robinson Jr., R.B. (1984). Measuring organizational performance in the absence of objective measures: The case of the privately-held firm and conglomerate business unit, *Strategic Management Journal*, 5(3), pp. 265–273.

Dobbs, M. and Hamilton, R.T. (2007). Small business growth: Recent evidence and new directions, *International Journal of Entrepreneurial Behaviour & Research*, 13(5), pp. 296–322.

Dowling, M.J. and McGee, J.E. (1994). Business and technology strategies and new venture performance: A study of the telecommunications equipment industry, *Management Science*, 40(12), pp.1663–1677.

Forsman, H. (2013). Environmental innovations as a source of competitive advantage or vice versa? *Business Strategy and the Environment*, 22(5), pp. 306–320.

Forsman, H. and Annala, U. (2011). Small enterprises as innovators: Shift from a low performer to a high performer, *International Journal of Technology Management*, 56(2–4), pp. 154–171.

Forsman, H. and Temel, S. (2011). Innovation and business performance in small enterprises. An enterprise-level analysis, *International Journal of Innovation Management*, 15(3), pp. 641–665.

Forsman, H., Temel, S. and Uotila, M. (2013). Towards sustainable competitiveness: Comparison of the successful and unsuccessful eco-innovators, *International Journal of Innovation Management*, 17(3).

Freel, M.S. (2000). Do small innovating firms outperform non-innovators? *Small Business Economics*, 14(3), pp. 195–210.

Freel, M. (2005). The characteristics of innovation-intensive small firms: Evidence from "Northern Britain", *International Journal of Innovation Management*, 9(4), pp. 401–429.

Geroski, P. and Machin, S. (1992). Do innovating firms outperform non-innovators? *Business Strategy Review*, 3(2), pp. 79–90.

Heunks, F.J. (1998). Innovation, creativity and success, *Small Business Economics*, 10(3), pp. 263–272.

Horbach, J. (2008). Determinants of environmental innovation — New evidence from German Panel data sources, *Research Policy*, 37(1), pp. 163–173.

Jarvis, R., Curran, J., Kitching, J. and Lightfoot, G. (2000). The use of quantitative and qualitative criteria in the measurement of performance in small firms, *Journal of Small Business and Enterprise Development*, 7(2), pp. 123–134.

Kannebley, S. Jr., Sekkel, J.V. and Araujo, B.C. (2010). Economic performance of Brazilian manufacturing firms: A counterfactual analysis of innovation impacts, *Small Business Economy*, 34(3), pp. 339–353.

Lechner, C. and Gudmundsson, S.V. (2014). Entrepreneurial orientation, firm strategy and small firm performance, *International Small Business Journal*, 32(1), pp. 36–60.

Lilischkis, S. (2013). Policies for High Growth Innovative Enterprises. In Report: Tsipouri. L., Georghiou, L. and Lilischkis, S. (Eds), *Report on the 2013*

ERAC Mutual Learning Seminar on Research and Innovation Policies. (European Commission: Brussels). Online. Available at: http://ec.europa.eu/ research/innovation-union (Accessed 15.2.2015).

Lotti, F., Santarelli, E. and Vivarelli, M. (2009). Defending Gibrat's law as a long-run regularity, *Small Business Economics*, 32(1), pp. 31–44.

Mason, G., Bishop, K. and Robinson, C. (2009). *Business growth and innovation: The wider impact of rapidly-growing firms in UK city-regions.* Research Report. (NESTA, London). Online. Available at: http://www.nesta.org.uk/ publications/business-growth-and-innovation (Accessed 04.10.2013).

McKelvie, A. and Wiklund, J. (2010). Advancing firm growth research: A focus on growth mode instead of growth rate, *Entrepreneurship, Theory and Practice*, 34(2), pp. 261–288.

Neumark, D., Wall, B. and Zhang, J. (2011). Do small businesses create more jobs? New evidence for the United States from the national establishment time series, *The Review of Economics and Statistics*, 93(1), pp. 16–29.

OECD (2002). *High-growth SMEs and employment.* (OECD, Paris). Online. Available at: http://www.oecd.org/industry/smes/2493092.pdf (Accessed 15.12.2013).

OECD (2010). *High-Growth Enterprises: What Governments Can Do to Make a Difference.* OECD Studies on SMEs and Entrepreneurship. (OECD Publishing).

Oke, A., Burke, G. and Myers, A. (2007). Innovation types and performance in growing UK SMEs, *International Journal of Operations and Production Management*, 27(7), pp. 735–753.

Phelps, R., Adams, R. and Bessant, J. (2007). Life cycles of growing organizations: A review with implications for knowledge and learning, *International Journal of Management Reviews*, 9(1), pp. 1–30.

Porter, M. (1985). *Competitive Advantage: Creating and Sustaining Superior Performance.* (The Free Press, New York).

Robson, P.J.A. and Obeng, B.A. (2008). The barriers to growth in Ghana, *Small Business Economics*, 30(4), pp. 385–403.

Rochina-Barrachina, M.E., Mañez, J.A. and Llopis, J.A. (2010). Process innovations and firm productivity growth, *Small Business Economics*, 34(2), pp. 147–166.

Roper, S. (1997). Product innovation and small business growth: A comparison of the strategies of German, UK and Irish companies, *Small Business Economics*, 9(6), pp. 523–537.

Shane, S. and Venkataraman, S. (2000). The promise of entrepreneurship as a field of research, *The Academy of Management Review*, 25(1), pp. 217–226.

Steffens, P., Davidsson, P. and Fitzimmons, J. (2009). Performance configurations over time: Implications for growth- and profit-oriented strategies, *Entrepreneurship, Theory and Practice*, 33(1), pp. 125–148.

Storey, D.J. and Greene, F.J. (2010). *Small Business and Entrepreneurship.* (Pearson Education, Essex).

Tang, Y.-C. and Liou, F.-M. (2010). Does firm performance reveal its own causes? The role of Bayesian inference, *Strategic Management Journal*, 31(1), pp. 39–57.

Tidd, J. (2001). Innovation management in context: Environment, organization and performance, *International Journal of Management Reviews*, 3(3), pp. 169–183.

Verhees, F.J.H.M., Meulenberg, M.T.G. and Pennings, J.M.E. (2010). Performance expectations of small firms considering radical product innovation, *Journal of Business Research*, 63(7), pp. 772–777.

Weinzimmer, L.G., Nystron, P.C. and Freeman, S.J. (1998). Measuring organizational growth: Issues, consequences and guidelines, *Journal of Management*, 24(2), pp. 235–262.

World Bank (2012). *World Development Report 2013: Jobs.* (World Bank, Washington, DC).

York, J.G. (2009). Pragmatic sustainability: Translating environmental ethics into competitive advantage, *Journal of Business Ethics*, 85(1), pp. 97–109.

Chapter 5

Towards Superior
or Lost Competitiveness

5.1 Introduction

Traditionally small businesses have been dependent on local economies. However, in today's globalized and uncertain business environment they should compete not only with their local competitors but also with international ones. Due to the fact that competition among small businesses has radically tightened over the years, their survival is increasingly dependent on created and sustained competitive advantage [Gunasekaran *et al.*, 2011]. It has commonly been argued that small firms should innovate in order to remain competitive. These innovations offer opportunities for small firms to create competitive advantages which help strengthen their competitiveness resulting in better business performance. Hence, innovation, competitive advantage, competitiveness and business performance are closely connected concepts.

Competitive advantage is defined as an ability of a firm to create more economic value than the marginal competitor in the market [Peteraf and Barney, 2003] and for that reason, competitive advantage will generate above-average returns [Peteraf, 1993]. According to Barney [1991], a firm has competitive advantage when its strategy for value creation is not simultaneously implemented by its current or potential competitors.

He continues that competitive advantage is sustained if these competitors are not able to duplicate the benefits of this strategy. However, Peteraf and Barney [2003] point out that competitive advantage is a fundamental but not necessarily sufficient element for achieving superior performance. Nevertheless, if a firm has gained superior performance, it has more likely created some sort of competitive advantage [Powell, 2001].

In regard to competitiveness, Stigler [1987, p. 531] explains that it emerges when "*two or more parties strive for something that all cannot obtain*". Thus, competitiveness is a relative concept in which the competing parties are compared with each other. At firm-level competitiveness has commonly been explained through the well-balanced combination of price and quality for achieving success in competition. According to Feurer and Chaharbaghi [1994], competitiveness depends on customer values and the abilities of a firm to respond to them within its business environment. This means that a firm is distinguished from competitors through the lenses of its customers. Hence, competitiveness should result in long-term performance related to its competitors leading, in the best scenario, to market-related and efficiency-related growth [cf. Man *et al.*, 2002; Forsman *et al.*, 2013].

The question of how different kinds of innovators have achieved growth or decline was discussed in the previous chapter. This chapter focuses on the question of how small firms have achieved long-term performance. Thus, the relationship between innovation and performance are approached from another angle. The different kinds of growers are identified first and thereafter the elements and characteristics of their competitiveness are examined.

In this examination, innovation is regarded as a potential source of competitive advantage while competitiveness is considered as an ability of a firm to exploit this competitive advantage by competing successfully with its competitors. This leads to a general proposition that superior business performance emerges from superior competitiveness which in turn emerges from superior competitive advantage and innovation is an input for creating this competitive advantage [cf. Powell, 2001; Peteraf and Barney, 2003; Greve, 2009; Forsman *et al.*, 2013].

The next section discusses competitiveness in small firms. It identifies the characteristics and dimensions of competitiveness. Thereafter, the different kinds of growers as well as decliners are identified. This will be followed by analyzing their competitiveness. Finally, in order to locate similarities and differences in the competitiveness patterns, the extreme pairs of the different kinds of growers and decliners are compared.

5.2 Competitiveness in Small Firms

The models for competitive advantage and competitiveness have commonly been created based on the evidence from large firms. However, the characteristics of small firms differ in many aspects from their large counterparts. For example, small firms do not have similar market power, they are more vulnerable to external conditions, their abilities to respond to changes in the market can be limited, they possess scarce resources, their managerial style is less formalized and finally, their processes and systems are unstructured [Man *et al.*, 2002; Carvalho and Costa, 2014]. On the other hand, the small size provides some advantages such as flexibility, higher ability to adapt and improve, customer and learning orientation as well as an ability to implement change quickly [Salavou *et al.*, 2004; Forsman and Rantanen, 2011]. These characteristics affect the way how small firms face competition. For that reason, it has been argued that the models developed to large firms cannot be directly applied to smaller ones [Man *et al.*, 2002].

Prior literature provides a few general models for constructing competitiveness in the context of small business. While regarding the elements of models there is some variation, they commonly include internal and external factors as separate constructs [Horne *et al.*, 1992; Man *et al.*, 2002; Gunasekaran *et al.*, 2011]. The internal factors comprise a number of firm-specific issues related to resources, systems, innovation, organizational behavior and culture, quality as well as managerial and entrepreneurial characteristics [Man *et al.*, 2002; Gunasekaran *et al.*, 2011]. Correspondingly, the external factors assess the business environment involving both reactive and proactive approaches. These include such issues as the availability of opportunities, threats of vulnerability, industrial differences, globalization, requirements for responsiveness and collaboration in business networks [Horne *et al.*, 1992; Man *et al.*, 2002].

In addition to the internal and external factors, the models bring in a variety of enabling constructs such as the use of technology, capital, location, marketing and long-term performance as a resource as well as an outcome [Man *et al.*, 2002; Gunasekaran *et al.*, 2011].

While prior literature provides quite unanimous answers to the question of what factors affect competitiveness, it provides a diversity of answers to the question of what are the best indicators to measure competitiveness. On the other hand, related to many of the factors presented above, it could be easier to assess competitiveness than measure it.

In the context of small business, a model developed by Buckley *et al.* [1988] has often been applied to measure competitiveness [see for example Man *et al.*, 2002; Guzmán *et al.*, 2012]. It suggests that competitiveness should be measured from three dimensions: competitive potential, competitive process and competitive performance. The indicators to measure competitive potential demonstrate the inputs allocated to a process, the performance indicators reflect the output of this process while the indicators to measure competitive process indicate efficiency between the input and the output [cf. Buckley *et al.*, 1988]. As can be noticed, all above dimensions are more related to the internal factors than the external ones.

Considering that in this chapter competitiveness is defined as an ability of a firm to transform the created competitive advantage to the above-average returns, competitive potential refers to the sources of competitive advantage, the ability of a firm to transform competitive advantage into the above-average returns refers to the competitive process and the above-average returns refer to performance as an outcome. Thus, it can be summarized that instead of being a static concept showing how competitive a firm is, competitiveness is a process in continuous motion [Buckley *et al.*, 1988; Man *et al.*, 2002].

Regarding competitive potential, such indicators as technological abilities, access to capital and other resources, staff productivity and quality are used to assess the richness and diversity of sources for competitive advantage [Buckley *et al.*, 1988; Gunasekaran *et al.*, 2011]. In today's turbulent business environment innovation is considered as one of the vital sources of competitive advantage. Tidd [2001] has identified how the type of innovation contributes to competitive advantage. According to him, the disruptive innovations can lead to a new value proposition that can even rewrite the rules of industry while the radical innovations can result in novel products and services that may enable premium pricing. Tidd [2001] continues that the complex innovations can lead to barriers due to the difficulty in learning and finally, the continuous incremental innovation may result in the continuous movement of the cost and performance frontier.

From these innovation types, the radical and continuous incremental innovations are the more typical sources of competitive advantage in small firms [Forsman, 2011]. According to Christensen and van Bever [2014], these two types of innovations contribute to competitiveness by improving performance and efficiency. Instead, due to the high risk level, uncertain time scale for getting returns as well as the lack of technological knowledge, capital and other resources, small firms only seldom develop disruptive innovations. These innovations that can be new even to the whole world contribute not only to the creation of new markets but also to the creation of new jobs [Christensen and van Bever, 2014]. With respect to complexity, while learning orientation is one of the strengths in small firms, they, however, tend to follow their conventional pathways. Hence, small firms may engage in developing this type of innovation in the networked business environment.

The activities of transforming competitive potential into competitive performance belong to management [Buckley *et al.*, 1988; Gunasekaran *et al.*, 2011]. In small firms this is especially true due to the highly influential role the owner-managers play in goal setting, decision making and business activities [Man *et al.*, 2002]. In small firms the management tasks are agglomerated into the hands of very few individuals, quite often there is only one individual, the owner-manager of the firm who decides how the business activities will be accomplished.

Lobontiu and Lobontiu [2014] found that these entrepreneurial managers have difficulties in sharing responsibility, thus having a tendency to keep their control over the business activities, especially regarding the production, sales and marketing operations. Thus, a particular challenge that should be solved when a small firm starts to grow is the need to broaden the management team by more professional managers [Breslin, 2010]. Nevertheless, in order to ensure both the exploration and exploitation of business opportunities, the entrepreneurial management must be balanced with professional management [Churchill and Lewis, 1983]. Broadening the management team can be a painful process and for that reason, Breslin [2010] highlights the importance of the socialization process when integrating the new arriving managers into a growing small business.

However, in addition to the managerial qualities, also the skills and knowledge of employees should not be underestimated. Thus, the human factors play a key role in the competitive process and for that reason the indicators should focus on measuring capabilities. In addition to knowledge and skills, the goal orientation of owner-managers has been found to have a high impact on this process [Chawla *et al.*, 1997; Man *et al.*, 2002].

On the other hand, it has also been found that competitiveness is created along with the accumulative process in which the level of prior competitiveness predicts the level of future competitiveness [Gill and Biger, 2012; Forsman, 2013; Forsman *et al.*, 2013]. This means that the firms that already have achieved high competitiveness, through this experience possess better abilities to improve and maintain their competitiveness level. On the other hand, high prior competitiveness may have resulted in improved business performance. This in turn improves the abilities of a firm to allocate adequate resources for the competitive process affecting the competitive potential. Correspondingly, low prior competitiveness could mirror poor capacity to create competitive advantage [Wagner, 2009].

The above reflects that small firms can learn to create competitiveness and grow. Macpherson [2005] emphasizes the key role of managers in learning how to grow. This demands knowing how to act for finding solutions to the particular challenges. In the context of small business, learning and knowing should be integrated into their daily activities. However, small firms tend to follow their conventional pathways and thus, the past experiences may also inhibit learning [Macpherson, 2005; Forsman *et al.*, 2013]. Hence, success is associated with the managerial and organizational abilities to explore and adapt as well as to break out of existing path dependencies while failure is associated with the lack of these abilities [Macpherson, 2005].

On the basis of the above, prior performance reflecting the learning history may be an appropriate indicator to measure the competitive process of a firm to transform its competitive potential into competitive performance. It may also reflect the abilities of a firm to allocate inputs to this process.

In regard to performance, it has been measured by using a variety of indicators. Buckley *et al.* [1988] emphasize that competitive performance should be measured by applying outcome-based indicators. This justifies the use of market-related and efficiency-related indicators. These commonly include accounting-based lagging indicators used to measure post performance and growth [cf. Tidd, 2001; Wagner and Schaltegger, 2003; Forsman *et al.*, 2013]. The lagging indicators have been criticized due to the fact that they do not communicate how these outcomes have been achieved [Kaplan and Norton, 1996]. Nevertheless, the performance drivers are often firm-internal and for that reason, they are difficult to observe, especially in the context of small business [cf. Wagner and Schaltegger, 2003; Jarvis *et al.*, 2000].

Profitability and productivity are typical indicators used to measure efficiency-related competitiveness [cf. Buckley *et al.*, 1988; Bonifant *et al.*, 1995; Tidd, 2001] while sales growth, market share as well as revenues from the current and new markets are used to measure market-related competitiveness [cf. Bonifant *et al.*, 1995; Porter and van der Linde, 1995; Tidd, 2001]. However, these indicators should not be used as the single measures. If the market-related indicator is used alone, it could result in high competitiveness values for the firms that have increased their market share or sales by dumping the prices, an unprofitable expansion as an outcome. On the other hand, if the efficiency-related indicator is used alone, it could result in high competitiveness values for the firms that have under-exploited their competitive opportunities reflecting weaknesses in the competitive process [cf. Davidsson *et al.*, 2009]. For that reason, a combination of the efficiency-related and market-related indicators should be applied to measure competitive performance.

Wagner [2009] proposes that also the risk-related aspect should be considered when assessing competitiveness at firm-level. The risk-related indicators demonstrate how attractive the firm is through the lenses of investors reflecting the opportunities for getting access to capital and the cost of it. The risk-related competitiveness can be measured for example by equity ratio or debt ratio. The ratio of total assets financed by debt increases the risks of investors [King and Lenox, 2001; López *et al.*, 2007]. The registered intellectual property rights especially in knowledge and technology-intensive small firms also affect the attractiveness of a firm as an investment opportunity decreasing the risks.

Finally, Man *et al.* [2002] have identified that small businesses have four basic characteristics that qualify for competitiveness: long-term orientation, controllability, relativity and dynamism.

The first characteristic, long-term orientation in competitiveness means that a firm should stay competitive for a longer period [Man *et al.*, 2002]. Hence, this rules out unprofitable market-related growth in which products and services are sold underpriced compared with the incurred expenses [Buckley *et al.*, 1991]. According to Gunasekaran *et al.* [2011], this demands organizational behavior with an emphasis on the long-term strategy as well as on the managerial characteristics to ensure high quality in products and services.

The second characteristic, controllability, emerges from the resource-based view in which competitiveness is based on the resources and capabilities controlled by a firm [Man *et al.*, 2002]. According to Barney [1991], these resources should be valuable, rare, difficult to imitate and difficult to substitute.

The third characteristic, relativity, arises from the competitive strategy approach [Porter, 1985]. It reflects how competitive a firm is compared with the other firms in its industry [Feurer and Chaharbaghi, 1994]. Therefore, competitiveness should be measured by using the relative indicators [Corbett and Wassenhove, 1993; Man *et al.*, 2002].

Finally, the fourth characteristic, dynamism demonstrates how a firm transforms its competitive potentials through the competitive process into competitive outcomes. Thus, competitive advantage does not last forever [Barney, 1991; Horne *et al.*, 1992]. Dynamism refers to the abilities of a firm to create new competitive advantages for staying competitive for a longer period of time. [Man *et al.*, 2002.]

Based on the above, it can be summarized that the single indicators alone or the set of indicators of a single dimension fail to capture the characteristics and dynamics of competitiveness [Buckley *et al.*, 1988].

External environment

Characteristics of competitiveness

Fig. 5.1.   Framework for measuring competitiveness.

Instead, both quantitative and qualitative indicators are needed to measure or assess competitiveness. Based on the above aspects, in this chapter the competitiveness of small firms will be assessed by applying the model consisting of five elements (see Figure 5.1): the factors of external environment, competitive potential, competitive process, competitive performance and the characteristics of competitiveness.

Regarding the external environment, it includes the factors related to the industrial sector reflecting technological abilities, customer requirements and typical investments in RD activities [Pavitt, 1984]. In addition, satisfaction with location and the usage of regional development and consulting services will be assessed.

Competitive potential is assessed based on the resources allocated to the competitive process. This includes both internal resources as well as the resources gained through socializing and collaboration with external partners. In addition, an access to financing has an important role for ensuring adequate competitive potential in small firms. The opportunities for getting access to capital increases if the firm's abilities to meet its future obligations are under control. This means that the financial structure of a firm should be in balance between the shareholder's equity and debt used to finance the assets of a firm. Thus, in the following assessments, the debt-to-equity ratio is used as an indicator to measure risk-related competitive potential.

The competitive process is assessed based on the capabilities to orchestrate this process. In addition, the diversity of innovation activities are considered to reflect the nature of competitive process. It has also been found that the prior abilities to transform the competitive potentials to competitive performance play a key role in this process. For that reason, the prior abilities for creating market-related, efficiency-related and risk-related success are included in this dimension.

The competitive performance of a firm demonstrates the outcome of the competitive process. As mentioned earlier, competitiveness should be based on long-term orientation positing that a firm should stay competitive for a longer period [cf. Man *et al.*, 2002]. This means that market-related growth should be profitable. For that reason, competitive performance is measured by a combination of market-related, efficiency-related and risk-related indicators.

Finally, the characteristics of competitiveness are assessed based on four aspects vision, controllability, relativity and dynamics [cf. Man *et al.*, 2002]. Regarding the vision, several scholars emphasize the importance of long-term vision and goal orientation in small firms. Future orientation and the existence of long-term vision is explored based on the intentions of firms to develop their capabilities for preparing the future. Controllability is assessed by comparing the balance between internal and external resources. Relativity is measured by comparing the competitiveness of a firm against the other firms. Finally, the dynamics is assessed based on the abilities of a firm to stay competitive for a longer period of time.

The above model will be applied for assessing the competitiveness of the different kinds of growers. Prior to it, these growers are indentified in the next sections. The competitive input and the competitive process are assessed based on information collected for the period of six years from 2003 to 2008. Instead, competitive performance is measured for the period of four years from 2009 to 2012.

5.3 Different Kinds of Growers

The smaller firms tend to grow faster than the larger firms [e.g., Lotti *et al.*, 2009; Neumark *et al.*, 2011]. However, this growth has a tendency to congeal once the firms have achieved the size that allows them to run their business activities and survive in the market in which they operate [Lotti *et al.*, 2009]. Especially new start-ups are growing fast in order to achieve the size needed to operate successfully in their industries [Dobbs and Hamilton, 2007; Mason *et al.*, 2009] and it seems that the new high-tech firms are reaching this efficient size more easily than the other firms [Nunes *et al.*, 2010].

It has been suggested that small firms follow several pathways to grow. However, there are only a few studies that have identified these pathways. Delmar *et al.* [2003] have carried out one of them for exploring how small firms reach high growth. They identified seven grower profiles from which four are dominated by small- and medium-sized firms: super-absolute growers, super relative growers, erratic one shot growers and employment growers.

The super absolute growers exhibit high absolute growth in both sales and employment while *the super relative growers* have a very strong but more or less erratic progress regarding both sales and employment. While super absolute growers are found from the knowledge-intensive manufacturing businesses, the super relative growers are located within the knowledge-intensive service businesses. Although the third profile, *the erratic one-shot growers* consists of firms with a declining size, they have experienced one very strong growth year. Finally, *the employment growers* are expanding in terms of the number of employees while the other growth indicators do not show similar progress for them. The erratic one-shot growers as well as the employment growers are located in the small services businesses characterized by low knowledge-technology intensity. [Delmar *et al.*, 2003.]

The above profiles bring in the importance of resilience and sustainability in identifying the different kinds of growers. In addition, the firm-related and business environment-related factors are emphasized. Nevertheless, it should be noted that the above profiles are identified by studying only the high growers. At the same time it excludes the majority of small firms in the examination. This has been criticized as a limited approach. This chapter aims to identify also the other types of growers. The next section, however, starts by focusing on the high growers.

While the growth patterns introduced by Delmar *et al.* [2003] have been used to identify the different kinds of growers, the following comparisons enhance our understanding about the characteristics of these growers and their abilities to compete. This will be done by analyzing the competitiveness of these firms by using a framework presented in

Section 5.2 to assess their competitive potential, competitive process and competitive performance. In addition, the external factors that may affect competitiveness of a firm will be identified.

5.3.1 High growers versus high decliners

The high growers are distinguished from other small businesses based on two attributes. They should have achieved high growth in the firm size and this growth should have continued over an intensive period of time [OECD, 2010]. However, the researchers have different opinions about the degree of growth and the length of growth period that qualifies a high-growth firm [Furlan *et al.*, 2014].

The OECD [2010] defines that the high-growth firms have on average greater than 20% growth per annum during a three-year period and the size of firms should be at least 10 employees at the beginning of the observation period. The three-year observation period has been criticized due to the fact that it is too short for exploring the changes in growth. Another reason for criticism is that the above definition excludes the smallest firms with fewer than 10 employees from the examinations. In most countries, more than 90% of all firms have fewer than 10 employees [Eurostat, 2013; World Bank, 2012].

Both researchers and policy-makers have been especially interested in the high-growth firms due to their significant contribution to job creation and employment. Given the limitations above, it is natural that the share of high-growth firms is relatively low. It has been estimated that approximately 6% of all firms are high-growth firms and they account for 35% to 50% of new jobs created by the firms having at least 10 employees [Bravo Biosca, 2010; OECD, 2010]. When examining the high-growth firms in Europe and the US, it has been identified that on average a high-growth firm multiplies its employment by more than 2.5 times over a three-year period [Bravo Biosca, 2010].

High growth has commonly been connected with high knowledge-technology intensity, young age and small size [Henrekson and Johansson, 2010; Mason and Brown, 2013; Coad *et al.*, 2012]. Nevertheless, the recent studies demonstrate that the high-growth firms exist in all industries, in all size categories and in all age groups (especially if growth is measured by value growth, employment growth favor younger firms) [cf. Anyadike-Danes *et al.*, 2009; Coad *et al.*, 2012]. Other characteristics that are identified among the high-growth firms are innovative and entrepreneurial behavior, management qualities, export orientation, internationalization and focus on growth instead of profitability [Moreno and Casillas, 2007; Du and Temouri, 2014]. Innovation has been considered as a very important element of their competitive potential while the capabilities of management, export orientation and internationalization activities are needed for transforming these innovations into competitive performance [cf. Mason and Brown, 2013].

Based on the above, the high-growth firms have been identified as one grower profile the competitiveness of which should be explored further. Nevertheless, while scholars and policy-makers have been especially interested in the high-growth firms, they have ignored an opposite type, the firms that are declining fast. It has been recognized that the high-growth firms create a high proportion of new jobs but they also are subject to a high level of turnover [Dobbs and Hamilton, 2007]. Also Coad and Hölzl [2009] point out that turbulence in job creation and job destruction is generated by the fast-growing and fast-declining firms. For that reason, the high decliners are selected to be compared with high growers.

By adopting the definition of the OECD [2010], a firm is classified as a high grower if its sales have increased by more than 20% during three consecutive years between the period starting in 2004 and ending in 2008. Correspondingly, a firm is considered as a high decliner if its sales have decreased by more than 20% during three consecutive years. Totally 40 firms, 20 high growers and 20 high decliners were selected for this comparison. The competitiveness patterns of these two growers are presented in Table 5.1.

Regarding the external environment, the high growers are most often the manufacturing businesses while the high decliners are more often the service businesses. An interesting finding is that within both the high growers and the high decliners their knowledge-technology intensity varies indicating that the high-growth firms as well as the high-decline firms can emerge in all sectors. Instead, the high growers are more often located in the urban regions while the high decliners are located equally between the urban and rural areas.

Table 5.1.   Competitiveness of high growers and high decliners.

	High grower	**High decliner**	**Sig.**
External environment			
Sector	Manufacturing	Service	*
Knowledge-tech intensity	Varies	Varies	
Location	Urban	Rural/Urban	
Satisfaction to environment	Average	Below average	
Usage of regional services	Average	Low	
Competitive potential			
Internal resources	High	Low	∧
Abilities to finance hidden innovation	Above average	Low	**
External resources	High	Above average	*
Risk-related potential	Average	Average	
Competitive process			
Innovation capabilities	High	Above average	
Radical innovation activities	High	Average	
Incremental innovation activities	Average	Average	
Prior market-related abilities	High	Low	***
Prior efficiency-related abilities	Average	Below average	∧
Prior risk-related abilities	Average	Below average	*
Competitive performance			
Market-related performance	High (relative)	Low	***
Efficiency-related performance	Average	Below average	*
Risk-related performance	Average	Below average	
General characteristics of competitiveness			
Vision	Varies	Short-term	
Controllability	Average	Low	
Relativity	Average	Below average	
Dynamics	Average	Below average	
Other aspects			
Over-representation in the innovation performer profile	Radical and High Performers	Low and Radical Performers	
Job creation/destruction (%)	+44.8	−31.6	

Note: Sig. indicates whether the differences between high growers and high decliners are statistically significant.

What comes to competitive potential, it is quite strong within the high growers while the high decliners have lower values. The high growers allocate a substantial amount of resources to internal development activities and their abilities to finance hidden innovation activities are above average. Especially the potential for exploration activities is reinforced through collaboration. However, the risk-related potential of high growers is only average indicating that they may have experienced difficulties in getting access to external funding needed to finance their radical innovation activities and growth.

The competitive process of high growers is characterized by the high degree of innovation capabilities, diversified innovation activities and prior abilities to build market-related competitiveness. These should provide a fertile ground for transforming their competitive potential into competitive performance. However, the empirical evidence demonstrates that absolute sales growth in these firms has started to slow down while relative sales growth is still high. Hence, despite the promising competitive potential and competitive process, the high growers have not been able to transform their high potential into high long-term performance. In fact, during the past four years their competitiveness has been in the declining trend. Nevertheless, compared with the other firms in this sample. At the end of 2012, the high growers still have high values in terms of relative market-related competitiveness and average values for efficiency-related and risk-related competitiveness.

An interesting finding is that the Radical Performers are over-represented within the high growers as well as the high decliners. Also the High Performers are over-represented within the high growers while the Low Performers have over-representation within the high decliners.

The policy-makers have been especially interested in these firms due to their contribution to new job creation. Somewhat conflicting with this assumption, in this comparison the empirical evidence demonstrates that the high growers have experienced much lower employment-related growth than the other growing profiles in this comparison. The number of employees has increased by 44.8% over a 10-year period between 2002 and 2012. Correspondingly, within the high decliners the number of employees has decreased by 31.6%.

Prior literature points out that high growth is a temporary phase. For example, Coad *et al.* [2013] recognized that only seldom does a firm persist its high-growth during the period of four consecutive years. It has been found in prior studies that high growth soon turns to moderate growth. This seems to be the situation also with the high growers in this sample. Their high growth period took place between the years of 2004 and 2008. It turned, however, into moderate absolute growth during the period of 2009–2012.

The above findings are supported by a general assessment of the characteristics of competitiveness. It reveals that the characteristics neither within the high growers nor within the high decliners are similar to the optimal patterns introduced in prior literature. Within the high growers the time span of vision varies and other aspects of competitiveness are close to average.

When searching the competitive items that distinguish the high growers from the high decliners, the non-parametric tests reveal that there exist statistically significant differences in sector, internal and external resources, abilities to finance hidden innovation and prior abilities to build market-related, efficiency-related and risk-related competitiveness. The highest significance levels were identified to prior abilities to build competitiveness and the abilities of firms to finance hidden innovation. This supports the arguments that competitiveness is created in the accumulative learning process and for that reason it takes time to achieve superior competitiveness.

In general, the empirical evidence suggests that the high growers have quite a long way to go for achieving sustained competitiveness. However, much more radical efforts are needed from the high decliners to achieve even short-term competitiveness.

5.3.2 Sustainable growers versus sustainable decliners

As mentioned earlier, high-growth episodes are not persistent, and only rarely does high growth tend to remain over a longer period of time [Coad *et al.*, 2012]. Instead, in a few years it seems to turn to moderate growth [Daunfeldt and Halvarsson, 2013]. The changes can be dramatic especially within the micro-sized firms while the firms larger in size are growing more smoothly.

Driven by these findings, a debate is emerging whether the major contribution to employment is provided by the high growth firms or the small firms characterized by incremental expansions. For example, Dobbs and

Hamilton [2007] argue that it is sustained growth that creates jobs and well-being. In general, compared with the high-growth firms, these moderate but sustained growers are larger in size, they are characterized by strong customer orientation and stable customer relationships, their growth aspirations are ambitious but less aggressive than within the high-growth firms, they have created their capabilities during a longer period of time and finally, they are responding quickly not only to the market-related changes but also to the efficiency-related changes [Moreno and Casillas, 2007; Forsman *et al.*, 2013].

Simon [2009] identified a specific group of businesses entitled as hidden champions. The hidden champions are firms that produce inconspicuous products but in the market they belong to leaders. While these firms have ambitious growth goals, they do not seek fast and high growth. Instead, they want to achieve continuous and modest growth [Bravo Biosca, 2010]. According to Lilischkis [2013], these highly innovative firms are important for creating jobs and wealth and thus, they are more worthwhile than the firms characterized by high but unsustainable growth. Despite a large share of this kind of growers, the researchers and the policy-makers have paid less attention to them. Hence, it is not only high growth but also sustained growth that creates new jobs and well-being for the society.

The strategic management literature discusses sustainability based on the temporary nature of competitive advantage. It points out that competitive advantage is achieved for a short period of time only and thus, it is ephemeral in nature [D'Aveni *et al.*, 2010; Sirmon *et al.*, 2010]. For example, Thomas and D'Aveni [2009] found that the stability of performance has decreased over time reflecting that temporary competitive advantage is becoming more common. Thus, competitive advantage should be sustained through a series of temporary advantages over time [cf. Wiggins and Ruefli, 2005]. This demands that competitiveness is sustained along with an accumulative process that derives from the continuous development of the competitive advantage of a firm [cf. Chen *et al.*, 2011; Forsman *et al.*, 2013]. However, this is not always enough. D'Aveni *et al.* [2010] refer to prior literature by asking whether also good luck is needed for achieving sustainable competitive advantage in the uncertain and unpredictable environment. Nevertheless, luck is out of the firm's control and thus, it is difficult to orchestrate [Barney, 1986].

While prior studies provide some empirical evidence to identify the sustainable growers, the evidence regarding sustainable decliners is scarce. Therefore, the second pair selected for the comparison is the sustainable growers and the sustainable decliners. The sustainable growers are firms that have experienced above average growth and this growth has continued from year to year. Correspondingly, the sustainable decliners are the firms that have confronted a below average decline and also this progress has continued during the same eight-year period.

Hence, a firm is classified as a sustainable grower if its sales have increased by more than 10% during five consecutive years during the period of 2004 to 2008. Correspondingly, a firm is considered as a sustainable decliner if its sales have decreased by more than 10% during five consecutive years.

Table 5.2 shows the competitiveness patterns of the sustainable growers and the sustainable decliners. A large share of the sustainable growers are manufacturing businesses located in the urban regions. They are satisfied with their business environment and the opportunities it offers to them. A high number of these firms represent the scale-intensive businesses that have their competences in the coordination of production processes in order to fulfill the needs of their price-sensitive customers.

The competitive potential of sustainable growers is close to average with one exception. They possess high abilities to finance hidden innovation. The sustainable growers reinforce their internal resources through collaboration especially for strengthening efficiency-related competitiveness. While their competitive potential is somewhat average, the competitive process of sustainable growers is more convincing. They possess high levels of innovation capabilities and high prior abilities to create market-related and risk-related competitiveness. This is accompanied by above average abilities to create efficiency-related competitiveness. Their radical and incremental innovation activities are in balance but the diversity of them is close to average.

The sustainable growers have transformed their moderate competitive potential into high market-related competitiveness and average efficiency-related and risk-related competitiveness.

When assessing the characteristic of competitiveness within the sustainable growers, Table 5.2 shows that the characteristics are close to average. Only the relativity is quite high reflecting the fact that compared

Table 5.2.   Competitiveness of sustainable growers and sustainable decliners.

	Sustainable grower	Sustainable decliner	Sig.
External environment			
Sector	Manufacturing	Service	^
Knowledge-tech intensity	Average	Average	
Location	Urban	More rural	^
Satisfaction with environment	High	Low	**
Usage of regional services	High	Below average	
Competitive potential			
Internal resources	Average	Average	
Abilities to finance hidden innovation	High	Low	***
External resources	Average	Above average	
Risk-related potential	Average	Average	
Competitive process			
Innovation capabilities	High	Below average	
Radical innovation activities	Average	Average	
Incremental innovation activities	Average	Average	
Prior market-related abilities	High	Low	***
Prior efficiency-related abilities	Above average	Below average	***
Prior risk-related abilities	High	Low	***
Competitive performance			
Market-related performance	High	Low (relative)	***
Efficiency-related performance	Average	Low	**
Risk-related performance	Average	Low	**
Characteristics of competitiveness			
Vision	Medium-term	Medium-term	
Controllability	Below average	Average	
Relativity	Above average	Low	
Dynamics	Average	Low	
Other aspects			
Over-representation in the innovation performer profile	Incremental Performer	Low Performer	
Job creation/destruction (%)	+217.4	−36.1	

Note: Sig. indicates whether the differences between the sustainable growers and decliners are statistically significant.

with other firms, they are coping quite well in terms of competitiveness. The combination of average characteristics of competitiveness and high market-related competitive performance is somewhat conflicting due to the fact the sustainable growers have sustained their competitiveness lasting, so far, at least eight years. This gives a reason to ask whether the high or above average values regarding the characteristics of competitiveness reveal sustained long-term competitiveness.

When comparing the differences in competitiveness between the sustainable growers and the sustainable decliners, the statistically significant differences were located regarding the sector, location, satisfaction with business environment, abilities to finance hidden innovation and prior abilities to build competitiveness. In a similar vein to the comparison between the high growers versus the high decliners, also between the sustainable growers and the sustainable decliners the highest significance level was identified regarding the prior abilities to build competitiveness and abilities to finance hidden innovation. The sustainable growers have learnt to build competitiveness and turn it into sustained growth. On the other hand, the sustainable decliners have learnt to survive in very challenging conditions.

Finally, Dobbs and Hamilton [2007] argue that it is not high growth but sustainable growth that creates new jobs. The empirical evidence of this chapter demonstrates that the sustainable growers have tripled their size during the period of 10 years. The number of their employees has increased by 217.4%. Hence, it is reasonable to assume that this group of firms will benefit the whole society in terms of new job creation. Based on the sample used in this book, these firms are more likely to be located within the Incremental Performers. Correspondingly, the Low Performers accommodate a high proportion of sustainable decliners. The number of their employees has decreased by 36.1% by 2012 compared with 2003.

5.3.3 Sales growers versus profit makers

One challenge regarding the above profiles is that they ignore the fact whether growth is profitable or not. For example, Davidsson *et al.* [2009] argue that there is a risk that growth with low profits is only temporary in nature and after a short period of time both the profitability and growth of these firms will drop below the average. Expansion demands financial resources and while low profits reflect that the firm does not have internal resources to be allocated for growth, it may also have difficulties to get external resources for financing its expansion. Furlan *et al.* [2014] emphasize that the internal resources have a key role for sustaining the growth process at the beginning of the expansion period while the growth process inverts the situation and brings later in also the need for external resources.

An important question is how to achieve profitable growth? Davidsson *et al.* [2009] suggest that in order to achieve profitable growth, a firm should exploit the opportunities that have a good match with its resources. In the case that a firm tries to seize other opportunities for growth, it may destroy rather than create value. On the other hand, if the firm under-exploits its optimal growth opportunities, it may reach high profitability based on the partially exploited competitive opportunities. Hence, this suggests that in order to maximize its profitable growth, a firm should establish a competitive advantage based on efficiency-related and market-related strengths.

However, all firms cannot balance or do not want to balance these two types of competitiveness. This leads to select the third pair for the comparison: a sales grower, that is a firm with high sales growth with low profitability and a profit maker, that is a firm with low sales growth with high profitability. The former refers to the firms that have achieved high market-related growth but their efficiency-related performance is low while the latter refers to the firms that that have achieved high efficiency-related performance but their market-related growth is low.

These profiles are consistent with the profiles identified by Davidsson *et al.* [2009], and entitled as the growth firms and the profit firms. As regards the growth firms, their low profitability reflects that they are less likely to have established resource-based advantages and transformed them into superior value creation for the benefits of customers. Hence, their expansion may require under-pricing or expensive marketing efforts to attract the customers facing equal offerings from competitors [Peteraf and Barney, 2003]. What comes to the profit firms, the resource-based view suggests that they have gained an ability to create and appropriate value above the average compared with their industrial sector. However, the development of this kind of advantage has taken its toll in terms of market-related growth. [Davidsson *et al.*, 2009.]

Hence, a firm is classified as a sales grower if it belongs to the highest quarter in terms of combined relative and absolute sales growth during the four-year period between 2005 and 2008 and during the same period it had a below average profit level. On the contrary, a firm is classified as a profit maker if it belongs to the highest quarter in terms of profit ratio while its sales growth was below average during the same period of four years. The competitiveness patterns of the sales growers and the profit makers are provided in Table 5.3.

In regard to the external environment, the sales growers are more often the manufacturing businesses while the profit makers are the service businesses. While the knowledge-technology intensity of sales growers is below average, it is above average among the profit makers. The high share of the sales growers are supplier-dominated firms characterized by very price-sensitive customers. They mainly adopt technology developed by others and make it function in their own activities. Correspondingly, the profit makers accommodate a high share of firms characterized by dependence on information networks. They provide knowledge-intensive business services to their performance-sensitive customers.

In regard to competitive potential, both the sales growers and the profit makers possess somewhat average internal and external resources. Instead, they differ in terms of risk potential. Risk-related competitive potential is high among the profit makers while it is low within the sales growers.

While the sales growers and the profit makers have quite similar competitive potential, their competitive processes differ significantly. The sales growers possess high prior abilities to build market-related competitiveness but low abilities to create efficiency-related and risk-related competitiveness. The patterns among the profit makers are reverse. They possess high prior abilities to build efficiency-related and risk-related competitiveness but low abilities to create market-related competitiveness.

Both the sales growers as well as the profit makers have used their one-sided abilities to transform their competitive potential to one-sided competitive performance. The sales growers have strengthened their relative market-related competitiveness while their efficiency-related and

Table 5.3. Competitiveness of sales growers and profit makers.

	Sales grower	**Profit maker**	**Sig.**
External environment			
Sector	Manufacturing	Service	**
Knowledge-tech intensity	Below average	Above average	^
Location	Urban	Rural/urban	
Satisfaction with environment	Above average	Average	
Usage of regional services	Average	Low	
Competitive potential			
Internal resources	Average	Below average	
Abilities to finance hidden innovation	Below average	Average	^
External resources	Above average	Below average	
Risk-related potential	Low	High	***
Competitive process			
Innovation capabilities	Average	Low	
Radical innovation activities	Average	Below average	
Incremental innovation activities	Average	Below average	
Prior market-related abilities	High	Low	***
Prior efficiency-related abilities	Low	High	***
Prior risk-related abilities	Low	High	***
Competitive performance			
Market-related performance	High (relative)	Low (relative)	
Efficiency-related performance	Low	High	***
Risk-related performance	Low	Above average	***
Characteristics of competitiveness			
Vision	Medium	Short-term	
Controllability	Average	Average	
Relativity	Varies	Varies	
Dynamics	Varies	Varies	
Other aspects			
Over-representation in the innovation performer profile	Low Performer	High Performer	
Job creation/destruction (%)	+102.2	−5.3	

Note: Sig. indicates whether the differences between the sales growers and the profit makers are statistically significant.

risk-related competitiveness has remained low. Correspondingly, the profit makers have strengthened their efficiency-related competitiveness. Instead, their risk-related competitiveness is in declining trend while they have slightly improved their market-related competitiveness in terms of absolute sales growth. Hence, this result indicates that the firms tend to follow their conventional pathways. These profiles have a 10-year-long history of emphasizing unilaterally either market-related competitiveness or efficiency-related competitiveness. Instead, in order to achieve long-term competitiveness in which market-related and efficiency-related competitiveness is balanced, they have a long way to go.

When assessing the characteristics of competitiveness within the sales growers and the profit makers, it was recognized that the sales growers have a medium-term vision while the profit makers have a shorter time span for their future plans. Instead, the other characteristics of these two profiles are quite similar. Considering that the profit makers have managed to improve slightly their weak area, market-related competitiveness, there arises again the question of whether the high values in characteristics reflect high competitiveness or whether the average values comprise a better indicator to reveal it.

When comparing competitiveness between the sales growers and the profit makers, statistically significant differences were located regarding the sector, knowledge-technology intensity, risk-related potential, abilities to finance hidden innovation and prior abilities to build competitiveness. The highest significance level was identified regarding the prior abilities to build competitiveness and risk-related potential. Through their learning history, both the sales growers and the profit makers possess prior abilities in the fields in which their competitiveness is high.

This strengthens the proposition that competitiveness is achieved through learning and hence, small firms should learn to build competitiveness. However, they should avoid one-sided learning for enhancing only their strengths. They should also learn to improve the fields in which they have weaknesses. The Low Performers that are characterized by low or even non-existing innovation activities and weak innovation management practices are over-represented within both the sales growers and the profit makers. The above characteristics comprise a combination that offers a limited number of learning opportunities to these firms.

Finally, quite often the firms are encouraged to start their expansion by growing in terms of sales. Based on the results of this empirical evidence this could be a slow pathway towards long-term competitiveness. In addition, quite often high growth in sales has been linked with growth in employment. The employment figures reveal that the sales growers have expanded by 102.2% during the past 10 years. Instead, the profit makers do not contribute to job creation at all. In these firms the number of employees has decreased by 5.3%.

5.3.4 Job creators versus job destructors

The benefits of small business growth for the society will realize through the contribution these firms make to employment. However, the recent studies highlight that all small firms do not provide the same contribution to the economy. As mentioned earlier, it is expected that a comparatively small share of firms do create a high share of new jobs for boosting employment [Neumark *et al.*, 2011; Coad *et al.*, 2013; Mason and Brown, 2013]. While this type of growth is not an expressed goal for the small business owners, it is of high interest to policy-makers.

As mentioned earlier, it is a commonly shared understanding that the high-growth firms provide the highest contribution to new job creation. On the other hand, they are also the most potential job destructors [Dobbs and Hamilton, 2007; Coad and Hölzl, 2009]. Also the differences in productivity have been found to affect the dynamics in employment. However, while the current literature introduces conflicting views about job creation, it provides only scant evidence about job destruction. For that reason, a natural selection for the fourth pair is the job creators and the job destructors. The job creators are the firms that have possessed a growing trend in terms of the number of employees while the job destructors have possessed a declining trend.

Thus, a firm is classified as a job creator if it is on the top-20 list based on high growth in paid salaries during the period from 2005 to 2008. Correspondingly, a firm is classified as a job destructor if it is found on the lowest-20 list. The competitiveness patterns of job creators and job destructors are presented in Table 5.4.

Regarding the sector, a bit higher share of job creators is located in the manufacturing sectors than in the service sectors while the job decliners are found more evenly from both sectors. The knowledge-technology intensity varies in these firms and thus it can be assumed that both the job creators and the job destructors may emerge from

Table 5.4.   Competitiveness of job creators and job destructors.

	Job creator	Job destructor	
External environment			
Sector	Manufacturing	Manufacturing/ service	*
Knowledge-tech intensity	Varies	Varies	
Location	More urban	Rural/urban	
Satisfaction with environment	High	Below average	^
Usage of regional services	High	Low	^
Competitive potential			
Internal resources	Below average	Low	
Abilities to finance hidden innovation	High	Below average	***
External resources	Average	Average	
Risk-related potential	Average	Average	
Competitive process			
Innovation capabilities	High	Above average	
Radical innovation activities	Average	Low	
Incremental innovation activities	Above average	Average	
Prior market-related abilities	High	Low	***
Prior efficiency-related abilities	Above average	Below average	*
Prior risk-related abilities	Above average	Low	***
Competitive performance			
Market-related performance	High (relative)	Low (relative)	***
Efficiency-related performance	Average	Average	
Risk-related performance	Average	Below average	
Characteristics of competitiveness			
Long-term vision	Medium-term	Medium-term	
Controllability	Above average	Low	
Relativity	Varies	Below average	
Dynamics	Average	Below average	
Other aspects			
Over-representation in the innovation performer profile	High Performer	Low Performer	
Job creation/destruction (%)	+157.7	−45.4%	

Note: Sig. indicates whether the differences between the job creators and the job destructors are statistically significant.

all business fields. The job creators are more commonly running their businesses in urban regions and they are highly satisfied with their business environment. Correspondingly, the job destructors are located in both the rural and urban areas and their satisfaction with the business environment is much lower.

What comes to the competitive potential, it seems to be close to average within both the job creators and the job destructors. There is one exception. The job creators possess high abilities to finance hidden innovation while the job destructors have below average abilities. In order to compensate low internal resources allocated to innovation activities, the job creators collaborate for enhancing their development-related and efficiency-related competitive potential. Instead, the job destructors distinguish from other firms by having a high emphasis of collaboration on socializing and the personal relationships of the owner-managers.

While there are only minor differences in competitive potential, the differences are much larger regarding the competitive process. The job creators possess the higher abilities to transform their competitive potential into competitive performance. While the job creators possess high or above average prior abilities to create all three types of competitiveness, the job destructors are struggling within all three dimensions. However, the job destructors have managed to gain a slightly improving trend in their competitiveness indicating that they have overcome the immediate risk of failure.

As regards the characteristic of competitiveness, the job creators are on average. Correspondingly, the characteristics within the job destructors show quite poor figures.

Finally, when searching the characteristics that distinguish the job creators from the job destructors, the non-parametric tests reveal statistically significant differences regarding external environment, competitive process as well as competitive performance. More precisely, the differences are located in sector, satisfaction with environment, usage of regional services, abilities to finance hidden innovation and prior abilities to create competitiveness. Finally, the job creators outperform the job destructors in terms of market-related competitive performance.

When exploring the contribution of these growers to employment and job creation, it was identified that during a 10-year period between 2002 and 2012 the number of employees has increased by 157.7% within the job creators while within the job destructors it has declined by 45.4%. Thus, the job creators comprise a promising group of firms to offer new job opportunities in the economy. The job creators are more likely found among the High Performers while the job destructors may locate within the Low Performers.

5.3.5 Super growers versus super decliners

Finally, the most common indicators used to measure growth are market-related, efficiency-related and employment-related indicators. The pairs selected above represent the different kinds of combinations regarding competitiveness. There is also a need to combine these indicators. This justifies the choice of the fifth pair, the firms that belong to the highest quarter and the firms that belong to the lowest quarter in terms of all three growth dimensions. The firms that during the period of four years in 2005–2008 have achieved very high market-related, efficiency-related and employment-related growth are entitled as super growers while the firms that during the same period have encountered very low market-related, efficiency-related and employment-related growth are entitled as super decliners.

The super growers and the super decliners are quite similar to the profiles identified by Davidsson *et al.* [2009], and entitled as the stars and the poors. The stars are profitable growers that have successfully established a resource-based advantage for creating high value for their customers [Sirmon *et al.*, 2007]. Hence, the super growers characterized by sustained high profitable growth can be assumed to be able to maximize both value creation and value appropriation. Instead, the poors are performing below average on both growth and profits and it represents a profile that firms should avoid by all means [Davidsson *et al.*, 2009]. Hence, it is an interesting question of how the super growers have managed to establish their continuous multidimensional growth progress for a longer period of time. At least as interesting is the question of how the super decliners have eluded closing the business despite their continuous declining progress.

A firm is classified as a super grower if it belongs to the highest third in terms of market-related, efficiency-related and employment-related growth during the period of four years in 2005–2008. Thus, it is a firm that is expanding in terms of three dimensions. On the contrary, a firm is classified as a super decliner if it belongs to the lowest third in terms of market-related, efficiency-related and employment-related growth during the same period of four years.

The competitiveness patterns of these two growers are presented in Table 5.5.

Table 5.5.   Competitiveness of super grower and super decliner.

	Super grower	Super decliner	
External environment			
Sector	Varies	Service	
Knowledge-tech intensity	Varies	Varies	
Location	Urban	Rural/urban	
Satisfaction with environment	High	Below average	^
Usage of regional services	High	Average	
Competitive potential			
Internal resources	Above average	Above average	
Abilities to finance hidden innovation	High	Low	***
External resources	Average	Average	
Risk-related potential	Above average	Below average	**
Competitive process			
Innovation capabilities	High	Low	
Radical innovation activities	Average	Average	
Incremental innovation activities	Average	Average	
Prior market-related abilities	High	Low	***
Prior efficiency-related abilities	High	Low	***
Prior risk-related abilities	High	Low	***
Competitive performance			
Market-related performance	High (relative)	Low (relative)	***
Efficiency-related performance	Above average	Low	**
Risk-related performance	Above average	Below average	**
Characteristics of competitiveness			
Vision	Medium-term	Medium-term	
Controllability	Average	Above average	
Relativity	High	Low	
Dynamics	High	Low	
Other aspects			
Over-representation in the innovation performer profile	Incremental and High Performers	High Performer	
Job creation/destruction (%)	+222.7	−33.9	

Note: Sig. indicates whether the differences between the super growers and the super decliners are statistically significant.

Regarding the external environment, the super growers are almost equally located in the manufacturing and service businesses while the service businesses are over-represented within the super decliners. The knowledge-technology intensity of these both profiles varies indicating that there exists no typical business field for these exceptional growers or decliners. Instead, there are differences in location and satisfaction with the environment. The super growers are more often situated in the urban regions while the super decliners are found from both the rural and urban areas. The satisfaction and the usage of regional development and consultancy services are higher among the super growers than within the super decliners.

The results regarding the competitive potential are surprising. Both the super growers and the super decliners possess somewhat average internal and external resources allocated to the competitive process. Instead, their risk-related potential and abilities to finance hidden innovation differ. The super growers have more convincing financial structure indicating that they have an easier access to external funding. In addition, their abilities to finance hidden innovation are high.

There exist, however, larger differences in the competitive process. The super growers possess higher abilities to transform their competitive potential into competitive performance. The empirical evidence demonstrates that these firms have achieved high long-term market-related competitiveness above average efficiency-related and risk-related competitiveness. On the contrary, the super decliners continue their survival battle that, so far, has lasted for eight years.

When assessing the characteristics of competitiveness within the super decliners and the super growers, it was found that both of them have medium-term vision and average controllability over their competitive potential. Instead, relativity and dynamics are higher within the super growers indicating that they have sustained their competitiveness. In addition, they have better abilities to maintain this sustainability than the other firms in this sample.

Finally, when exploring the characteristics that distinguish the super growers and the super decliners, they were identified within the external environment, competitive potential, competitive process and competitive performance. Once again, the highest significance level was found related to prior abilities to build competitiveness, thus emphasizing the importance of learning perspective. In addition, the super growers possess significantly higher risk-related potential as well as better abilities to finance hidden innovation. Based on the empirical evidence, the super growers have learnt to build and strengthen their long-term competitiveness while the super decliners have learnt to tackle in a long-term survival battle.

While the super growers have more than doubled their profits and sales during a 10-year period, the number of employees has increased at the higher rate (222.7%). Within the super decliners the number of employees has declined by 33.9%. Hence, when searching the firms that provide high contribution to employment and job creation, the super growers are a potential location of these firms.

An interesting finding is that both the super growers and the super decliners are most likely found within the High Performers. This reflects that the growing and declining High Performers have similar abilities to develop innovations while they differ in terms of abilities to commercially exploit these innovations.

5.4 Chapter Summary

Competition among small businesses has radically tightened over the past years. For that reason, their survival depends increasingly on their abilities to create and sustain competitiveness. The aim of this chapter was to explore competitiveness within small firms by focusing on the questions of how small firms have achieved long-term competitiveness and how innovation is manifested in this process.

In this chapter, innovation was regarded as a potential source of competitive advantage while competitiveness was considered as an ability of a firm to exploit its competitive advantage by competing successfully with its competitors. Hence, it can be concluded that superior business performance emerges from superior competitiveness which in turn emerges from superior competitive advantage and innovation is one potential input for creating this competitive advantage.

However, it is challenging to measure competitiveness in the context of small business. One should decide what dimensions should be included in the framework, what indicators should be used and what time frame is appropriate for getting reliable results. While the vast majority of the models for measuring competitiveness are created based on the evidence gathered from large firms, the recent literature has started to develop frameworks that acknowledge also the characteristics of smaller firms. One of them is the model developed by Buckley *et al.* [1988] and further developed by Man *et al.* [2002]. It suggests that competitiveness should be measured from three dimensions: competitive potential, competitive process and competitive performance.

In this chapter the above three elements comprise the basic framework for constructing the competitiveness of small firms. Competitive potential refers to the sources of competitive advantage, the ability of a firm to transform competitive advantage into the above-average returns refers to the competitive process and the above-average returns refer to performance as an outcome. Due to the fact that the above elements are related to internal factors, also the external factors are included in the examination of this chapter. Finally, it has been identified that four basic characteristics qualify for competitiveness: long-term orientation, controllability, relativity and dynamism [Man *et al.*, 2002]. Also these should be explored when measuring the competitiveness of small firms. Thus, competitiveness is considered as a process that is in continuous movement.

Several scholars point out that small firms comprise a heterogeneous group of firms and there exist several pathways to success. Recognizing this heterogeneity, in this chapter the different kinds of growers and their opposite counterparts, decliners, were identified. Thereafter, the competitiveness of these grower-decliner pairs was analyzed and compared. The five grower pairs were selected for the comparison: high growers versus high decliners, sustainable growers versus sustainable decliners, sales growers versus profit makers, job creators versus job destructors and finally, super growers versus super decliners. The aim of comparison was to shed light on the characteristics and dynamics of competitiveness within the different kinds of growers. The model consisting of five elements; external factors, competitive potential, competitive process, competitive performance and finally, the characteristics of competitiveness, was applied for assessing the competitiveness of these growers.

Table 5.6 summarizes the distinguishing competitiveness features of the most promising growers while Table 5.7 presents the competitiveness figures of the less promising growers.

When looking at the most promising growers, Table 5.6 demonstrates that three growers out of five have quite similar competitiveness patterns.

Table 5.6. Summary of the competitiveness patterns of the most promising growers.

	Sustainable grower	Super grower	Job creator	Sales grower	High grower
External environment					
Sector	Manuf.	Varies	Manuf.	Manuf.	Manuf.
Knowledge-tech intensity	Medium	Varies	Varies	Low	Varies
Location	Urban	Urban	Urban	Urban	
Satisfaction with environment	High	High	High		
Usage of regional services	High	High	High		
Competitive potential					
Internal resources					High
Abilities to finance hidden innovation	High	High	High		
External resources					High
Risk-related potential				Low	
Competitive process					
Innovation capabilities	High	High	High		High
Radical innovation activities					High
Incremental innovation activities					
Prior market-related abilities	High	High	High	High	High
Prior efficiency-related abilities		High		Low	
Prior risk-related abilities	High	High		Low	
Competitive performance					
Market-related performance	High	High (R)	High (R)	High (R)	High (R)
Efficiency-related performance				Low	
Risk-related performance				Low	
Characteristics of competitiveness					
Vision	Medium	Medium	Medium	Medium	Varies
Controllability				High	High
Relativity		High	High		
Dynamics		High	High		
Other aspects					
Over-representation in the innovation performer profile	Incremental	High	High	Low	Radical, High
Job creation/destruction (%)	+217.4	+222.7	+157.7	+102.2	+44.8

Note: Empty cell reflects close to average values, (R) = relative only.

The sustainable and super growers as well as the job creators are all highly satisfied with their business environment, their competitive potential is average with one exception. They all possess high abilities to finance hidden innovation. While their competitive potential is mainly average, these

Table 5.7. Summary of the competitiveness patterns of the less promising growers.

	Profit maker	Sustainable decliner	Job destructor	Super decliner	High decliner
External environment					
Sector	Service	Service	Manuf.	Service	Service
Knowledge-tech intensity	High	Varies	Varies	Varies	Varies
Location	Varies		Varies	Varies	Varies
Satisfaction with environment		Low			
Usage of regional services	Low		Low		Low
Competitive potential					
Internal resources			Low		Low
Abilities to finance hidden innovation		Low		Low	Low
External resources					
Risk-related potential	High				
Competitive process					
Innovation capabilities	Low			Low	
Radical innovation activities			Low		
Incremental innovation activities					
Prior market-related abilities	Low	Low	Low	Low	Low
Prior efficiency-related abilities	High			Low	
Prior risk-related abilities	High	Low	Low	Low	
Competitive performance					
Market-related performance	Low (R)	Low (R)	Low (R)	Low (R)	Low
Efficiency-related performance	High	Low		Low	
Risk-related performance		Low	Low		
Characteristics of competitiveness					
Vision	Short	Medium	Medium	Medium	Short
Controllability			Low		Low
Relativity		Low		Low	
Dynamics		Low		Low	
Other aspects					
Over-representation in the innovation performer profile	Low	Low	Low	High	Low, Radical
Job creation/destruction (%)	−5.3	−36.1	−45.4	−33.9	−31.6

Note: Empty cell reflects close to average competitiveness, (R) = relative.

growers transform their limited resources efficiently to high competitive performance through the strengths in their competitive process. In general, they are very competitive compared with the other firms and especially the super growers and the job creators have abilities to sustain their competitiveness. The super growers and the job creators are most likely found among the High Performers while the sustainable growers may be located among the Incremental Performers.

An interesting finding is that these three growers, job creators, sustainable growers and super growers, provide a significant contribution to new job creation. During a 10-year period, the super growers and the sustainable growers have multiplied the number of their employees by 3.2 while the job creators are below them (2.6).

Also the two other profiles, the sales growers and the high growers share several similarities in their competitiveness patterns. First, their satisfaction with the business environment is average. Regarding the competitive process, their prior abilities to create market-related competitiveness are high, their competitive performance varies, controllability of competitive potential is high and finally, their contribution to job creation is lower compared with the other promising profiles. The Low Performers accommodate the highest proportion of sales growers while the Radical and High Performers accommodate the highest share of high growers.

Hence, it can be summarized that all promising growers seem to have from average to high values for all competitiveness items. The sales growers are an exception. They possess weaknesses in their prior abilities to create efficiency-related and risk-related competitiveness and during the period of 10 years they have not been able to improve these abilities. Another interesting feature is that among the promising growers the competitive potential seems to be at an average level. However, these small firms have their strengths in the competitive process and thus, these limited resources are efficiently transformed into competitive performance.

Prior literature emphasizes the importance of long-term vision in order to sustain competitiveness. The empirical evidence of this book does not provide support to this argument. The most competitive firms that already have sustained their competitiveness are characterized by medium-term vision and moderate goals for the future. It has also been a common assumption that the sectors characterized by high knowledge-technology intensity are more probably the sources of growing firms. Based on the results of this examination, there exists high variation in sectors suggesting that the growing firms can emerge from any sector. However, there exist some differences in sectors when comparing the extreme pairs against each other.

Finally, due to their expected contribution to new job creation the sales growers and the high growers are commonly treated as an important target group of public policies. However, when searching the employment figures during the period of 10 years, both the sales growers and high growers are far behind the other three promising growers in terms of employment effects. This examination suggests that the firms that have already sustained their competitiveness are more promising as the firms providing new job opportunities. On the other hand, this examination also suggests that the less aggressive growth and innovation goals may result in sustained growth within the established small firms.

Correspondingly, when looking at the less promising growers, Table 5.7 presents a reverse competitiveness pattern compared with the above most promising growers. There exists, however, one grower type that differs from the other less promising growers. The profit makers are characterized by their abilities to create long-term efficiency-related competitiveness while their abilities to create market-related abilities are weak. In addition, this is the only grower type that accommodates a high proportion of firms with high knowledge-technology intensity, especially those providing knowledge-intensive business services.

Instead, regarding the other competitiveness items, these five less promising grower types share several similarities. In general, all competitiveness items vary from low to average. When the most promising growers are characterized by average competitive potential and efficient competitive process, these less promising growers have a diverse pattern. Although they possess average competitive potential, they have weaknesses in their competitive process to transform this potential into performance.

It is also an interesting finding that within the less promising growers their innovation capabilities and diversity of innovation activities are at an average level, but their prior abilities to create competitiveness are weak. This formula seems to lead to weak competitiveness.

The highest proportion of declining firms is located among the Low Performers characterized by low innovation activities and non-existing innovation management practices.

Based on the above results, in can be concluded that average competitive potential is typical of the resource-scarce small firms. Instead, an efficient competitive process is necessary for transforming these limited resources into longer-term competitive performance. In addition, the results presented in this chapter demonstrate that there are several types of growers that follow their conventional pathways towards sustained or temporary competitiveness. Hence, learning seems to play a significant role in achieving and sustaining competitiveness. An interesting question is if this learning can be managed. This question of how small firms should manage their activities for learning to grow and prosper will be discussed in the next chapter.

References

Anyadike-Danes, M., Bonner, K., Hart, M. and Mason, C. (2009). *Measuring business growth*: *High-growth firms and their contribution to employment in the UK*. Research Report. (NESTA, London). Online. Available at: http://www.nesta.org.uk/assets/documents/measuring_business_growth_report (Accessed 04.10.2013).

Barney, J.B. (1986). Strategic factor markets: Expectations, luck, and business strategy, *Management Science*, 32(10), pp. 1231–1241.

Barney, J. (1991). Firm resources and sustained competitive advantage, *Journal of Management*, 17(1), pp. 99–120.

Bonifant, B.C., Arnold, M.B. and Long, F.J. (1995). Gaining competitive advantage through environmental investments, *Business Horizons*, 38(4), pp. 37–47.

Bravo Biosca, A.B. (2010). *Growth dynamics Exploring business growth and contraction in Europe and the US*. NESTA, Research report: November 2010. Online. Available at: http://www.nesta.org.uk/publications/growth-dynamics (Accessed 02.06.2014).

Breslin, D. (2010). Broadening the management team: An evolutionary approach, *International Journal of Entrepreneurial Behaviour & Research*, 16(2), pp. 130–148.

Buckley, P.J., Pass, C.L. and Prescott, K. (1988). Measures of international competitiveness: A critical survey, *Journal of Marketing Management*, 4(2), pp. 175–200.

Buckley, P.J., Pass, C.L. and Prescott, K. (1991). Foreign market servicing strategies and competitiveness, *Journal of General Management*, 17(2), pp. 34–46.

Carvalho, L. and Costa, T. (2014). Small and medium enterprises (SMEs) and competitiveness: An empirical study, *Management Studies*, 2(2), pp. 88–95.

Chawla, S.K., Pullig, C. and Alexander, F.D. (1997). Critical success factors from an organizational life cycle perspective: Perceptions of small business owners from different business environments, *Journal of Business and Entrepreneurship*, 9(1), pp. 47–58.

Chen, C.-J., Chang, C.-C. and Hung, S.-W. (2011). Influences of technological attributes and environmental factors on technology commercialization, *Journal of Business Ethics*, 104(4), pp. 525–535.

Christensen, C.M. and van Bever, D. (2014). The capitalist's dilemma, *Harvard Business Review*, 92(2), pp. 60–68.

Churchill, N.C. and Lewis, V.L. (1983). The five stages of small business growth, *Harvard Business Review*, 61(3), pp. 30–50.

Coad, A., Cowling, M. and Siepel, J. (2012). *Growth processes of high-growth firms in the UK*. Working paper no. 12/10. (NESTA, London). Online. Available at: http://www.nesta.org.uk/sites/default/files/growth_processes_of_high-growth_firms_in_the_uk.pdf (Accessed 29.06.2014).

Coad, A., Frankish, J., Roberts, R.G. and Storey, D.J. (2013). Growth paths and survival chances: An application of Gambler's Ruin theory, *Journal of Business Venturing*, 28(5), pp. 615–632.

Coad, A. and Hölzl, W. (2009). On the autocorrelation of growth rates, *Journal of Industry, Competition and Trade*, 9(2), pp. 139–166.

Corbett, C. and van Wassenhove, L. (1993). Trade-offs? What trade-offs? Competence and competitiveness in manufacturing, *California Management Review*, 35(4), pp. 107–122.

D'Aveni, R.A., Dagnino, G.B. and Smith, K.G. (2010). The age of temporary advantage, *Strategic Management Journal*, 31(13), pp. 1371–1385.

Daunfeldt, S.-O. and Halvarsson, D. (2013). *Are high-growth firms one-hit wonders? Evidence from Sweden.* KTH, Economics, Working Paper. Online. Available at: http://kth.diva-portal.org/smash/get/diva2:605656/FULLTEXT01.pdf (Accessed 8.6.2014).

Davidsson, P., Steffens, P. and Fitzsimmons, J. (2009). Growing profitable or growing from profits: Putting the horse in front of the cart? *Journal of Business Venturing*, 24(4), pp. 388–406.

Delmar, F., Davidsson, P. and Gartner, W.B. (2003). Arriving at high-growth firm, *Journal of Business Venturing*, 18(2), pp. 189–216.

Dobbs, M. and Hamilton, R.T. (2007). Small business growth: Recent evidence and new directions, *International Journal of Entrepreneurial Behaviour & Research*, 13(5), pp. 296–322.

Du, J. and Temouri, Y. (2014). High-growth firms and productivity: Evidence from the United Kingdom, *Small Business Economics* (in Press).

Eurostat (2013). *Structural Business Statistics*. Online. Available at: http://ec.europa.eu/eurostat/web/structural-business-statistics/overview (Accessed 14.02.2015).

Feurer, R. and Chaharbaghi, K. (1994). Defining competitiveness: A holistic approach, *Management Decision*, 32(2), pp. 49–58.

Forsman, H. (2011). Innovation capacity and innovation development in small enterprises. A comparison between the manufacturing and service sectors, *Research Policy*, 40(5), pp. 739–750.

Forsman, H. (2013). Environmental innovations as a source of competitive advantage or vice versa? *Business Strategy and the Environment*, 22(5), pp. 306–320.

Forsman, H. and Rantanen, H. (2011). Small manufacturing and service enterprises as innovators: A comparison by size, *European Journal of Innovation Management*, 14(1), pp. 27–50.

Forsman, H., Temel, S. and Uotila, M. (2013). Towards sustainable competitiveness: Comparison of the successful and unsuccessful eco-innovators, *International Journal of Innovation Management*, 17(3).

Furlan, A., Grandinetti, R. and Paggiaro, A. (2014). Unveiling the growth process: Entrepreneurial growth and the use of external resources, *International Journal of Entrepreneurial Behaviour & Research*, 20(1), pp. 20–41.

Gill, A. and Biger, N. (2012). Barriers to small business growth in Canada, *Journal of Small Business and Enterprise Development*, 19(4), pp. 656–668.

Greve, H.R. (2009). Bigger and safer: The diffusion of competitive advantage, *Strategic Management Journal*, 30(1), pp. 1–23.

Gunasekaran, A., Rai, B.K. and Griffin, M. (2011). Resilience and competitiveness of small and medium size enterprises, *International Journal of Production Research*, 49(18), pp. 5489–5509.

Guzmán, G.M., Gutiérrez, J.S., Cortes, J.G. and Ramírez, R.G. (2012). Measuring the competitiveness level in furniture SMEs of Spain, *International Journal of Economics and Management Sciences*, 1(11), pp. 9–19.

Henrekson, M. and Johansson, D. (2010). Gazelles as job creators: A survey and interpretation of the evidence, *Small Business Economics*, 35(2), pp. 227–244.

Horne, M., Lloyd, P., Pay, J. and Roe, P. (1992). Understanding the competitive process: A guide to effective intervention in the small firms sector, *European Journal of Operational Research*, 56(1), pp. 54–66.

Jarvis, R., Curran, J., Kitching, J. and Lightfoot, G. (2000). The use of quantitative and qualitative criteria in the measurement of performance in small firms, *Journal of Small Business and Enterprise Development*, 7(2), pp. 123–134.

Kaplan, R.S. and Norton, D.P. (1996). *The Balanced Scorecard: Translating Strategy into Action.* (Harvard Business School Press, Boston).

King, A.A. and Lenox, M.J. (2001). Does it really pay to be green. An empirical study of firm environmental and financial performance, *Journal of Industrial Ecology*, 5(1), pp. 105–116.

Lilischkis, S. (2013). Policies for High Growth Innovative Enterprises. In Report: Tsipouri. L., Georghiou, L. and Lilischkis, S. (Eds), *Report on the 2013 ERAC Mutual Learning Seminar on Research and Innovation Policies.* (European Commission: Brussels). Online. Available at: http://ec.europa.eu/research/innovation-union (Accessed 15.2.2015).

Lobontiu, G. and Lobontiu, M. (2014). The owner-manager and the functional management of a small firm. *Procedia — Social and Behavioral Sciences*, 124, pp. 552–561.

López, M.V., Garcia, A. and Rodrigues, L. (2007). Sustainable development and corporate performance: A study based on the Dow Jones sustainability index, *Journal of Business Ethics*, 75(3), pp. 285–300.

Lotti, F., Santarelli, E. and Vivarelli, M. (2009). Defending Gibrat's law as a long-run regularity, *Small Business Economics*, 32(1), pp. 31–44.

Macpherson, A. (2005). Learning how to grow: Resolving the crisis of knowing, *Technovation*, 25(10), pp. 1129–1140.

Man, T.W.Y., Lau, T. and Chan, K.F. (2002). The competitiveness of small and medium enterprises. A conceptualization with focus on entrepreneurial competencies, *Journal of Business Venturing*, 17(2), pp. 123–142.

Mason, G., Bishop, K. and Robinson, C. (2009). *Business growth and innovation: The wider impact of rapidly-growing firms in UK city-regions*. Research Report, (NESTA, London). Online. Available at: http://www.nesta.org.uk/publications/business-growth-and-innovation (Accessed 04.06.2014).

Mason, C. and Brown, R. (2013). Creating good policy to support high-growth firms, *Small Business Economics*, 40(2), pp. 211–225.

Moreno, A.M. and Casillas, J.C. (2007). High-growth SMEs versus non-high-growth SMEs: A discriminant analysis, *Entrepreneurship & Regional Development, An International Journal*, 19(1), pp. 69–88.

Neumark, D., Wall, B. and Zhang, J. (2011). Do small businesses create more jobs? New evidence for the United States from the national establishment time series, *The Review of Economics and Statistics*, 93(1), pp. 16–29.

Nunes, P.M., Serrasqueiro, Z., Mendes, L. and Sequeira, T.N. (2010). Relationship between growth and R&D intensity in low-tech and high-tech Portuguese service SMEs, *Journal of Service Management*, 21(3), pp. 291–320.

OECD (2010). *High-Growth Enterprises: What Governments Can Do to Make a Difference*. OECD Studies on SMEs and Entrepreneurship. (OECD Publishing).

Peteraf, M.A. (1993). The cornerstones of competitive advantage: A resource-based view, *Strategic Management Journal*, 14(3), pp. 179–191.

Peteraf, M.A. and Barney, J.B. (2003). Unraveling the resource-based tangle, *Managerial and Decision Economics*, 24(4), pp. 309–323.

Pavitt, K. (1984). Sectoral patterns of technical change: Towards a taxonomy and a theory, *Research Policy*, 13(6), pp. 343–373.

Porter, M. (1985). *Competitive Advantage: Creating and Sustaining Superior Performance*. (The Free Press, New York).

Porter, M.E. and van der Linde, C. (1995). Toward a new conception of the environment-competitiveness relationship, *Journal of Economic Perspectives*, 9(4), pp. 97–118.

Powell, T.C. (2001). Competitive advantage: Logical and philosophical considerations, *Strategic Management Journal*, 22(9), pp. 875–888.

Salavou, H., Baltas, G. and Lioukas, S. (2004). Organizational innovation in SMEs: The importance of strategic orientation and competitive structure, *European Journal of Marketing*, 38(9/10), pp. 1091–1112.

Simon, H. (2009). *Hidden Champions of the 21st Century: Success Strategies of Unknown World Market Leaders*. (Springer, London).

Sirmon, D.G., Hitt, M.A. and Ireland, R.D. (2007). Managing firm resources in dynamic environments to create value: Looking inside the black box, *Academy of Management Review*, 32(1), pp. 273–292.

Sirmon, D.G., Hitt, M.A., Arregle, J-L. and Campbell, J.T. (2010). The dynamic interplay of capability strengths and weaknesses: Investigating the bases of temporary competitive advantage, *Strategic Management Journal*, 31(13), pp. 1386–1409.

Stigler, G. (1987). *The New Palgrave. A Dictionary of Economics*, eds. Eatwell, J., Milgate, M. and Newman, P. (The MacMillan Press Limited, London), pp. 531–535.

Thomas, L.G. and D'Aveni, R. (2009). The changing nature of competition in the US manufacturing sector, 1950–2002, *Strategic Organization*, 7(4), pp. 387–431.

Tidd, J. (2001). Innovation management in context: Environment, organization and performance, *International Journal of Management Reviews*, 3(3), pp. 169–183.

Wagner, M. (2009). Innovation and competitive advantages from the integration of strategic aspects with social and environmental management in European firms, *Business Strategy and the Environment*, 18(5), pp. 291–306.

Wagner, M. and Schaltegger, S. (2003). How does sustainability performance relate to business competitiveness? *Greener Management International*, 44, pp. 5–16.

Wiggins, R.R. and Ruefli, T.W. (2005). Schumpeter's ghost: Is hypercompetition making the best of times shorter? *Strategic Management Journal*, 26(10), pp. 887–911.

World Bank (2012). *World Development Report 2013: Jobs.* (World Bank, Washington, DC).

Chapter 6

Innovation Engine to Foster Learning in Small Firms

6.1 Introduction

Due to the fact that innovation is considered as one of the main sources of competitive advantage, firms do their best to invest in innovation aiming at boosting their competitiveness. However, recent studies have identified that there exists a severe gap between what firms are targeting for and what they have gained through innovation [Birchall *et al.*, 2004; Forsman and Temel, 2014]. One reason for this could be the inadequate measurement practices. In order to manage successfully the innovation activities, they should be measured. However, it is easier to give this advice than to follow it. For example, Andrew *et al.* [2010], who carried out a survey within senior executives, identified that although innovation is a top priority within the respondents' firms, only 4 out of 10 of them are satisfied with their innovation measurement practices.

There are several ways how firms approach the measurement and management of their innovation activities. The traditional approach tends to measure the inputs of the innovation process in terms of RD investments and the outputs of the innovation process in terms of the number of new products or patent filings. This is, however, a limited approach. Measuring innovation demands a holistic framework starting from the creation of an idea and converting it into future business value. The process between inputs and outputs should be measured as well. [Forsman and Temel, 2014.]

Often firms focus on measuring what is easy to measure instead of what should be measured. Firms consider themselves the most effective at measuring the outputs of the innovation process while they are far less successful at monitoring the inputs allocated to the innovation process or the quality of this process [Andrew *et al.*, 2010].

Nevertheless, innovation measurement is a dyadic operation. An old phrase "*You cannot manage what you do not measure*" has been feeding the discussion on the advantages and disadvantages of performance measurement. While the performance management supporters explain that only the things that get measured are the things that get done, a typical answer from the opponents is that innovation is a complex, unpredictable and intangible process, and for that reason it is difficult to measure. Commonly, the opponents rationalize their arguments by explaining that measurement is a tool for command and control, not for innovation. According to this viewpoint, measurement can have negative impact on creativity leading to dysfunctional behavior and decreasing performance [cf. Amabile, 1998; Bititci *et al.*, 2006]. However, several scholars point out that in addition to directing decision making, the main goal of measurement should be learning [Davenport, 2006; Bititci *et al.*, 2012]. Hence, a measurement system should help firms learn to perform well.

Along with the analysis in this book, it has become evident that in the context of small firms it is learning that plays a key role in achieving and sustaining competitiveness and profitable growth. It raises a question of how small firms should measure and manage their activities in order to learn to grow. This chapter aims at contributing to the above question. It outlines how small firms can foster their learning through innovation activities for improving their competitiveness and chances for business success. This chapter starts by discussing the performance measurement in the context of small business. This will be followed by the identification of the system with the main dimensions and indicators for measuring innovation and competitiveness. Based on the above, the elements of the innovation engine are illustrated for small businesses.

6.2 Measuring Performance in Small Firms

Business performance is defined as an ability of a firm to achieve its business goals and produce the targeted outcome [Laitinen, 2002]. Innovation is one of the tools for achieving these business goals. On the other hand, better performing firms are more likely to innovate and allocate their resources to innovation activities [Cainelli *et al.*, 2006]. Hence, innovation performance is closely related with business performance. There exists a two-way cumulative and self-reinforcing connection between innovation success and business success.

According to Bourne *et al.* [2000], a comprehensive performance measurement system is needed to translate the needs of the main stakeholders into business goals and appropriate performance measures, and this system should be used for continuous improvement and learning. Despite the importance of performance measurement documented in management literature, within small firms the performance measurement activities have commonly been poor. These firms have some contextual characteristics that may inhibit measurement such as limited managerial capacity, the non-existence of formalized managerial processes, short-term strategic planning, lack of human and financial resources and reactive or even disinclined approach to measurement [Garengo *et al.*, 2005; Bititci *et al.*, 2012].

The above characteristics have led to a situation that small firms do not use performance measurement systems at all or they use them incorrectly [Garengo *et al.*, 2005]. This is understandable because the vast majority of these systems have been developed for the use in larger firms. For that reason, the systems are often too complicated and heavy to be applied in the context of small business. It has also been argued that small firms do not need performance measurement systems because all problems are visible and people get to know them without having such systems [Garengo *et al.*, 2005]. This view seems to consider that the performance measurement system is a tool for crisis management in small firms, the main priority of which is liquidity in short-term and survival in long-term [Jarvis *et al.*, 2000].

On the other hand, small firms running their businesses in local markets may possess needed agility, capability and information to prosper without having the systematic measurement practices [cf. Prashantham and Birkinshaw, 2008]. This is supported by Pedersen and Sudzina [2012] who studied performance measurement practices among the Danish firms and found that the firms operating in turbulent and unpredictable business environment are more likely to adopt a comprehensive performance measurement system.

Thus, in small firms performance measurement is only seldom the result of planned activity based on formal system. Instead, it is informal in nature and for that reason the involvement of employees is often low [cf. Hudson *et al.*, 2001; Garengo *et al.*, 2005]. In order to communicate new directions and strategic priorities with employees, measurement should take place regularly [cf. Melnyk *et al.*, 2010]. Despite this advice, performance measurement in smaller firms is not only ad hoc but it is also poorly aligned with strategic goals [Hudson *et al.*, 2001]. While reference to strategic goals is important, it is not anymore the starting point. The operational aspects and stakeholder orientation need increasing attention in the context of small business [Garengo *et al.*, 2005].

However, small firms are increasingly operating in a turbulent business environment and for that reason it is not enough to consider only the internal aspects when designing performance measurement. Simpson *et al.* [2012] criticize this traditional approach that treats firms as isolated black boxes in which business performance is monitored based on the number of firm-internal indicators with no connection with external environment in which these firms operate.

There is a need for a holistic measurement and management framework to drive the process that transforms ideas into profitable business [Adams *et al.*, 2006]. As a response to this need, the process-oriented performance measurement systems are increasing, especially among those developed to be used in the context of small business [Garengo *et al.*, 2005]. Cedergren *et al.* [2010] divided this process into three parts: enabling value, creating value and capitalizing value. The first part, enabling value, is related to the front-end innovation process during which the customer needs are identified and the decisions are made how a firm aims to respond to them. The second part, creating value, implements what has been decided and the finally, the third part, capitalizing value, is related to commercialization of the offerings developed. [Cedergren *et al.*, 2010.]

While the above framework has emphasis on innovation performance, Janssen *et al.* [2011] enhanced the process approach by separating the direct innovation-related output from business-related outcome. They used an input–process–output–outcome framework in which the input indicators provide information on the resources allocated to RD activities, process indicators measure the progress of a process, the output indicators demonstrate the direct results of the process and finally, the outcome indicators measure innovation success in the market [Brown and Svenson, 1988; Janssen *et al.*, 2011]. Thus, the above approach connects more closely innovation performance with business performance.

However, it should be noted that there is no clear beginning or end of the process. Therefore, the framework should be more system-oriented than just process-oriented. Bititci *et al.* [2012] point out that performance measurement should be considered as a social system and a learning system in the networked business environment. Bourne *et al.* [2000] identified three main phases for developing this kind of learning system. In the first phase the key business goals are identified and based on them the indicators are designed. This will be followed by the implementation phase during which the systems and routines are put into practice enabling the regular data collection and analysis of it. Finally, in the third phase the success of the implementation of strategic goals should be measured. In addition to this, the feedback of measures should be reflected for challenging the strategic assumptions.

At best, this process should lead to a self-reinforcing innovation-learning cycle, in which the reflection of innovation activities results in learning that leads to the identification of new even more challenging innovation goals. In turn, the implementation of these goals will through reflection lead to a new level of learning [cf. Forsman, 2009a]. In line with this, Cocca and Alberti [2010] summarize that the performance measurement system in the context of small business includes the system and its dynamics as an entity, the indicators used to measure performance and the practices and processes to measure the performance. In the next chapters, this kind of system is outlined accompanied with a set of potential indicators to be used in the context of small business.

6.3 The Innovation Engine for Small Firms

In order to be able to manage the innovation activities they have to be measured for getting guidance on decision making. Although measuring innovation is an important activity, it is not an easy activity. Especially capital-intensive radical innovation means often a jump into the unknown, which makes it difficult to assess the outcome in the early phases of development. Sometimes the indicators for measuring performance are misleading, for example having emphasis on the volume of ideas instead of the quality of them. This could lead to submission of a huge number of useless ideas. On the other hand, sometimes the indicators are one-sided measuring technological innovations based on the patent filings while neglecting the non-patentable innovations. However, if firms cannot determine the desired performance results, it is difficult, even impossible, to take appropriate managerial actions. [Forsman and Temel, 2014.]

The above challenges propose that a single measurement aspect, such as growth in sales, the number of presented ideas or patent filings, comprises a poor ground for the innovation performance system. In order to get a more balanced view of innovation activities, Janssen *et al.* [2011] point out the importance of a conceptual performance framework accompanied by a balanced set of innovation metrics including both qualitative and quantitative indicators for measuring innovation input and output as well as the process between these two.

Thus, measuring innovation is a complex task due to the multi-dimensional nature of innovation activities. Based on an extensive literature review, Adams *et al.* [2006] have developed a multi-dimensional model for measuring innovation. It consists of seven dimensions: organization and culture, knowledge management, innovation strategy, portfolio management, input management, project management, and commercialization.

By adopting quite similar dimensions, Forsman and Temel [2014] have presented a general approach that considers the innovation process as a system that acquires information and other resources, assimilates it and through a set of activities converts it to commercial ends [cf. Cohen and Levinthal, 1990]. The innovation goals, culture and structure of a firm provide the landscape for innovation and direct the innovation activities. In this system innovation and learning are intertwined in a way that innovation can be described as an embodiment of learning, and vice versa [Tran, 2008]. Hence, the innovation activities expose small firms to learning leading to a new level of capabilities. This in turn encourages small firms to set more ambitious innovation goals giving rise to an iterative process that fosters both learning and innovation activities.

In this chapter, the above framework for measuring innovation has been enhanced to the innovation engine that connects innovation with learning and the creation of competitiveness. The aim of the innovation engine is to demonstrate innovation success, not only based on the past success of innovation activities but also the potential future success of these activities. This system consists of six elements: external innovation landscape, internal innovation landscape, innovation potential, innovation process and activities, internal and external learning processes and finally, innovation performance. Figure 6.1 illustrates the elements of this system.

Due to the fact that there is no consensus on how to define innovation success, quite often it has been measured by using the indicators that are more appropriate for measuring business success. However, as discussed earlier, innovation success and business success are closely connected concepts. Alegre *et al.* [2009] separate these two aspects to innovation efficiency and innovation efficacy. According to them, innovation efficacy demonstrates the degree of innovation success while innovation efficiency reflects the efforts made to achieve that degree of success. In this innovation engine, the sixth element, innovation performance refers to

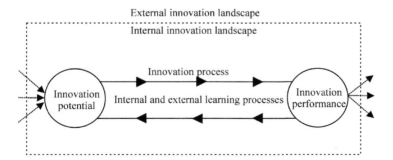

Fig. 6.1.   The elements of the innovation engine (Modified from Forsman and Temel [2014]).

innovation efficacy indicating the degree of innovation success while the rest of the elements are related to innovation efficiency reflecting the efforts made to achieve the desired level of innovation success.

The six elements of the innovation engine are introduced in detail in the following sub-chapters. While these elements provide answers to the question of what should be measured, it is also needed to search answers to the question of how the elements should be measured. This question will be answered by providing each element with a set of potential indicators that can be used in measurement.

6.3.1 External innovation landscape

In today's turbulent business environment all firms, small and large ones, deal with increasing change and tightening competition. When exploring innovation and growth in small businesses, the relevant questions to be considered are: "What impact does the business environment have on innovation and growth at firm-level?" It is clear that external environment and its economic situation affect small firms. A natural question is how systematically these firms are tracking the potential opportunities and threats of their business environment and analyzed the needed actions to respond to them. The systematic efforts are needed to monitor the changes in business environment [cf. Zollo and Winter, 2002].

Another aspect of external environment that should be considered is the functionality of environment in terms of infrastructure, the availability of knowledge and development services, the efficiency of regional innovation system, access to finance and finally, the regulatory environment [Ateljevic and Doorne, 2004; Aubert, 2005; Galindo and Micco, 2007; Robson and Obeng, 2008].

A well-functioning business environment provides incentives to small firms while the weaknesses may hamper their businesses. These issues affect the advantages or disadvantages of location. While small firms tend to have limited opportunities to influence their business environment [Christopherson and Clark, 2007; Hudson *et al.*, 2007], they should, however, be aware of the characteristics of their business environment. On the other hand, it is a firm that always makes a decision on the location of its business. For that reason, it would be useful to assess time to time how satisfied the firm is in its business environment and how satisfied its employees are in this environment as a working and living landscape.

Innovation is not anymore the domain of one firm. Instead, it is the matter of collaboration in business networks [Freel and Harrison, 2006]. Hence, small firms can enhance significantly their innovation potential through collaboration with partners from their external business environment.

The main motives of small firms to collaboration are to promote business development, create competitive advantage and boost overall profits and sales [Lin and Zhang, 2005; Mazzarol and Reboud, 2008]. Therefore, the external resources acquired through networking to these activities should be monitored. According to Nieto and Santamaria [2007], collaborative networks which include a variety of partners have a significant impact on innovation novelty. Based on this, one potential indicator for measuring external resources is the diversity of innovation partners. Nevertheless, small firms must also look for an optimal network structure and the right partners in order to get benefits out of collaboration [Rowley *et al.*, 2000]. If the main motives for external collaboration are access to external resources benefitting innovation activities, market expansion and efficiency, these aspects should be measured as well as the balance between them.

Table 6.1 summarizes the potential indicators for assessing the external innovation landscape discussed above.

As mentioned earlier, small firms have a limited influence on their external environment and their impact on policy-making seems to be lower than their economic impact [Christopherson and Clark, 2007]. One reason for this could be inertia in being involved in regional development activities as well as in policy-making. Another reason may be the fact that more visible large firms are expected to reflect the interests of the whole business community [Cooke *et al.*, 2005]. This challenge can be overcome by providing more information about the needs of small firms. In order to influence on their business environment especially regarding the functionality of it, the more active participation of small firms is needed in regional development activities and policy-making.

While the above-discussed external innovation landscape affects the opportunities of a firm to prosper, the internal innovation landscape

Table 6.1.   Potential indicators to assess external innovation landscape.

Indicators	Sources
Monitoring the business environment	
The extent to which the firm systematically tracks the changes in its business environment.	Zollo and Winter [2002]
Satisfaction with environment	
The extent to which the functionality of external environment meets the needs of a firm.	Ateljevic and Doorne [2004] Aubert [2005]
Firm satisfaction with external environment.	Galindo and Micco [2007]
Employee satisfaction with external environment.	Robson and Obeng [2008]
External resources	
The number and diversity of innovation partners.	Nieto and Santamaria [2007]
The extent to which the structure of external partners are in balance compared with the goals of a firm.	Rowley *et al.* [2000]
External resources to innovation activities.	Lin and Zhang [2005]
External resources to market-related activities.	Mazzarol and Reboud [2008]
External resources to efficiency-related activities.	Mazzarol and Reboud [2008]

provides a ground for it how efficiently a firm can exploit these opportunities. The next sub-chapter focuses on this question.

6.3.2   Internal innovation landscape

Innovation is a contextual phenomenon and the context either encourages or hampers innovation. If a small firm opts for innovation as its key success factor, it should ensure that its internal context supports innovativeness. This second element, internal innovation landscape illustrates the fertility of context at firm-level. It reflects the culture, commitment and direction of a firm to innovate. Dobni [2008] summarizes that this

Table 6.2. Indicators to assess internal innovation landscape.

Indicators	Sources
Behavior and culture	
How much the owner-manager spends his/her time on innovation.	Mankin [2007]
The extent to which it is supported to present new ideas and improved ways of doing things.	Anderson and West [1998]
The extent to which people are encouraged to take risks in a firm.	Dobni [2008]
The extent to which we always respond to new knowledge on customers and competitors.	Dobni [2008]
Intent to be innovative	
The existence of clear innovation goals.	Adams *et al.* [2006]
The effectiveness of the innovation goals in directing the activities.	Bessant [2003]
How well do the innovation goals match with business goals?	Bessant [2003]
Procedures to support innovativeness	
The extent to which the procedures and routines support the activities for achieving the innovation goals?	Bessant [2003]
The extent to which a firm makes it possible for employees to bend the rules.	Shane *et al.* [1995]
The extent to which the employees can participate in decision-making procedures.	Anderson and West [1998]
The extent to which employees share concern with the excellent quality of task performance.	Anderson and West [1998]

kind of context should include innovation and market-oriented behavior and culture, the intention to be innovative and the procedures should be in place to support innovativeness in a firm.

Table 6.2 presents some potential indicators on how these aspects can be measured in small firms.

Culture that supports innovation is engaged in such behavior as values creativity, risk-propensity, trust, freedom, collaboration and communication [Dobni, 2008]. On the other hand, the turbulence in business environment changes the way how the activities are managed and carried out in small firms. For example, in the ever-changing dynamic context, it will be difficult to find standard solutions that can be defined beforehand. For that reason, hierarchical structures become inefficient and it is needed to authorize decision making close to action [Molleman and Timmerman, 2003].

Hence, innovation inevitably demands changes through the transition in the work processes towards non-routine and non-repetitive direction characterized by the high level of interdependency between employees. In order to support innovativeness, the firms should empower employees to make decisions on the issues they are dealing with. On the other hand, this change demands that employees are willing to learn and they have tolerance for the high levels of ambiguity. Such a situation in which the innovation goals demand the activities resulting in radical change, it also increases the complexity of solutions. It is very unlikely that one person possesses the skills and knowledge that are required to master all the challenges. This situation brings in a need for collaboration, team working and efficient communication.

It is, however, not enough that the employees are ready for innovation challenges. In small firms the role of owner-managers and their commitment to innovation are crucial [cf. Hudson Smith and Smith, 2007; Cocca and Alberti, 2010]. In order to encourage innovative behavior, they should communicate their vision and goals for innovation being also supportive to champion the efforts and change in a firm [Muller *et al.*, 2005].

In the context of small business, the business goals should provide answer to the question of why to innovate while the innovation goals should answer the question of what to innovate. Hence, the innovation goals should direct the decision makers to select the innovation projects while innovation process and activities should provide an answer to the question of how to make it happen. Thus, the existence of innovation goals is a distinctive mark of the intention of a firm to be innovative [Kang and Lee, 2008]. On the other hand, it is also important to assess how well the innovation goals direct the activities in a firm and how they are aligned with general business goals [cf. Bessant, 2003]. The goals should also be in balance with the resources that can be allocated for achieving the goals.

All these aspects are easier to assess by using the qualitative reflective questions than to measure them based on quantitative indicators. The answers to qualitative questions in Table 6.2 demonstrate whether the respondents recognize the factors to be present or not, thus reflecting the existence of innovation goals and the fact how well the culture and procedures of a firm create a fertile internal landscape for innovation.

In summary, the common aspects for measuring the behavior and culture are related to the adaptiveness of staff to changes, their willingness to try new procedures and the autonomy of individuals in day-to-day decisions. The optimal external and internal environments provide a fertile ground for transforming innovation potential into innovation success. The next element of the innovation engine focuses on the question of how to measure and manage innovation potential.

6.3.3 Innovation potential

The third element, innovation potential, consists of tangible and intangible resources that can be allocated for innovation activities. These innovation enablers cover such items as idea generation, people and other internal resources. When measuring innovation potential, the emphasis has long been on financial indicators while the importance of soft indicators, such as skills and capabilities, has been more recently recognized [Adams *et al.*, 2006]. In order to ensure that both the hard and soft indicators are included, it would be better to focus on different types of resources separately, for example on financial resources, human resources, equipment and facilities. Table 6.3 summarizes the potential indicators for these aspects.

Regarding the financial resources, RD investments have been a frequently used indicator for measuring innovation. However, this indicator appears not to be appropriate for the majority of small firms that only seldom have formal RD activities and a separate RD budget.

However, adequate funding is a critical input into innovation process. Based on the empirical evidence used in this book, it seems that the majority of small firms are able to assess the percentage of sales that have been allocated to innovation activities.

Due to the fact that in small firms innovation development is integrated into their daily business operations being even hidden in nature, a logical question is whether they could afford to allocate extra resources in these activities. One answer can be found from their cash and profit figures. It can be assumed that a wealthy firm may have better abilities to hidden innovation than its indigent competitor. On the other hand, the lack of

Table 6.3.   Indicators to measure innovation potential.

Indicators	Sources
Financial resources	
Adequacy of funding.	Adams *et al.* [2006]
Percentage of sales allocated to innovation activities.	Forsman [2011]
How many times activities are delayed or canceled due to the lack of funding.	Davila *et al.* [2012]
Ability to allocate internal finance to innovation activities.	Forsman *et al.* [2013]
Human resources	
The number and diversity of people committed to innovation tasks.	Adams *et al.* [2006] Amabile [1998]
Adequacy of knowledge repository to respond to innovation challenges.	Damanpour [1992]
Prior abilities to develop innovations.	Forsman *et al.* [2013]
Prior abilities to successfully commercialize innovations.	Forsman *et al.* [2013]
Capture and generation of new ideas	
The number and the quality of ideas generated in a period.	Adams *et al.* [2006]
The diversity of the sources of new ideas.	Amabile [1998]
The number of ideas killed.	Hempel [2006]
The transparency of the actions for evaluating ideas and selecting the best ones for implementation.	
Equipment and facilities	
The value and adequacy of equipment.	Adams *et al.* [2006]
The value and adequacy of facilities.	Adams *et al.* [2006]

funding can be more easily recognized than the availability of it. One potential indicator is how often the lack of funding has obstructed innovation activities [cf. Davila *et al.*, 2012].

The human resources aspect has been commonly measured by the number of people committed to the innovation activities. The innovation studies have also demonstrated that a mix of knowledge and experiences these people possess influence innovation performance [Amabile, 1998]. Hence, the diversity of employees, in terms of their skills, experience, education or demographic factors, can be a useful indicator as well as the adequacy of the accumulated knowledge base of a firm [cf. Damanpour, 1992; Amabile, 1998]. On the other hand, along with this book, the empirical evidence has shown that the prior abilities of firms affect their innovation success. Therefore, these abilities should be considered as one item of human resources. Due to the fact that innovation includes both development and commercialization activities, it is needed to assess not only the abilities to develop innovations but also the abilities to commercialize successfully these innovations [cf. Forsman *et al.*, 2013].

The number and diversity of people affect the number and quality of ideas they produce to the innovation activities [cf. Amabile, 1998]. In addition, many of the ideas are captured outside the firm. Although external resources were discussed earlier in Section 6.3.1, it would be useful to monitor the number and diversity of sources of new ideas as an aspect of innovation potential. However, it should be kept in mind that, instead of volume, the quality of ideas is that matters. For that reason, firms should monitor not only the volume of the presented ideas but also the volume of killed ideas [Hempel, 2006]. In addition, it would be useful to clarify how the ideas are evaluated and how the best of them are selected for implementation.

What comes to equipment and facilities, it is a broad area with a variety of inputs from buildings to computers. These can be measured in terms of the value or adequacy of the resource [Adams *et al.*, 2006].

Finally this chapter was concerned with how to measure and manage innovation potential reflecting the resources allocated to innovation activities. The next chapter focuses on the question of how this potential is transformed into innovation performance.

6.3.4 Innovation process and activities

The fourth element, the innovation process and activities, flows through the phases of front-end, concept creation and back-end phase. The front-end phase focuses on exploring new opportunities and selecting the best ideas for solving the customer problems. In this phase the customer needs are identified and the decisions how to respond to them are made

[Cedergren *et al.*, 2010]. The concept creation is the implementation phase that is based on the made decisions turns the ideas into attractive concepts, for example products, services, processes or methods. Finally, the back-end phase focuses on commercialization that transforms these concepts into business success.

Hence, the innovation process and activities transform innovation potential into exploitable innovation outputs and business success. Two aspects arise for measuring innovation: the quality of the innovation process and the quality of the process output. [Forsman and Temel, 2014.] This chapter focuses on the quality of process while the quality of process output is discussed later when innovation performance element is presented (Section 6.3.6). The summary of the indicators and reflective questions to monitor and manage the quality of innovation process and activities has been presented in Table 6.4.

The efficiency of managing the innovation process has commonly been measured by comparing the original budget, schedule and planned goals

Table 6.4.   Indicators for managing the innovation process and activities.

Indicators	Sources
Quality of innovation process and activities	
The progress of innovation process/activities.	Adams *et al.* [2006]
The speed of innovation process.	Adams *et al.* [2006]
	Kessler and Chakrabarti [1996]
The extent and diversity of communication.	Adams *et al.* [2006]
	Damanpour [1992]
The adoption of organizational innovations	
The earliness, rate and speed of adoption.	Damanpour and Gopalakrishnan [2001]
	Subramanian and Nilakanta [1996]
Portfolio of innovation activities	
The extent to which resources are allocated to obtain optimal innovation portfolio?	Adams *et al.* [2006]
Is there a balance of portfolio between:	Adams *et al.* [2006]
— the high-risk and low-risk projects	Cooper *et al.* [1999]
— the radical and incremental projects	
— the projects enhancing existing business and new business	Mankin [2007]

with the realized figures. This means that the emphasis is on the progress of the innovation project. While this is justified as a process indicator, it could be inappropriate in small firms that do not organize their innovation activities to separate projects. In such cases it would be appropriate to use other indicators for example by assessing the innovation speed. The speed indicates how fast the innovation effort is completed. It can be measured in terms of the length of time for example between the conception of a new product and its introduction to customers [Kessler and Chakrabarti, 1996]. Due to the fact that small firms do not necessarily have formal project management and documentation procedures, informal communication is important for managing the innovation activities. Thus, the extent and diversity of communication are useful indicators, for example assessing the frequency of meetings, the number of contacts, and the degree of other stakeholders that are consulted on new ideas and how efficiently the employees are communicating with one another [cf. Damanpour, 1992; Adams *et al.*, 2006].

With respect to administrative and organizational innovations, the potential indicators are the earliness of adoption or the rate of adoption. The earliness of adoption reflects the timeline of the adoption decision in a firm compared to other firms [Subramanian and Nilakanta, 1996]. Correspondingly, the rate of adoption can be measured in terms of the total number of innovations adopted within a time interval and the percentage of innovations adopted from a pool of innovations within a given time period [Damanpour and Gopalakrishnan, 2001].

In addition to measuring the quality of a single innovation activity, the firm should also monitor its innovation portfolio. The portfolio consists of all innovation activities carried out by a firm. In order to translate the innovation goals into action, a firm should select and prioritize the activities to be carried out. The aim of the portfolio indicators is to measure the diversification of innovation activities and to manage the overall risk in firms. The questions that should be considered are whether the portfolio is optimal between risks and returns or between the radical and incremental innovation activities. It is also needed to assess whether the allocation of resources to activities is in balance compared with the innovation goals. [Forsman and Temel, 2014.] Finally, an important aspect for measuring the portfolio is to ensure that there is an optimal balance between the activities aiming at growing existing business and developing new business [Mankin, 2007].

The above indicators for measuring and managing the innovation process and activities are focused on the "hard aspects". Current literature has identified several soft aspects that drive innovation success such as learning, capability creation and collaboration. These are discussed in more detail in the next chapter.

6.3.5 Internal and external learning processes

Almost without exceptions, the innovation studies highlight the vital role of learning and knowledge-related processes for innovation success, especially if the firms are operating in the highly dynamic environments. Alegre *et al.* [2011] have separated learning into two processes: internal learning and external learning. Internal learning improves knowledge and abilities by using the internal resources and experiences of a firm. Correspondingly, external learning creates new knowledge and abilities through interaction with external partners. New knowledge created through external learning is an important input to an innovation process while new knowledge created through internal learning is also the output of this process.

Hence, learning and innovation builds a two-folded relationship. The innovation activities provide opportunities for learning by doing which in turn, improves the capabilities of a firm to innovate. The faster the firm learns, the faster it succeeds through innovation. Therefore, measuring innovation is also a way to measure the value of what a firm has learnt. This justifies the fifth element of the innovation engine, the learning processes. [cf. Forsman and Temel, 2014.]

In order to prosper firms should possess capabilities to transform innovation potential into innovations and further into competitiveness. Especially, the development of highly complex radical innovations requires a rich diversity of capabilities. Absorptive capacity that emphasizes collaborative learning has been offered as one solution for this [Cohen and Levinthal, 1990]. According to Zahra and George [2002], absorptive capacity reflecting the ability of a firm to identify, acquire and utilize external knowledge is critical to innovation success. This type of learning represents external learning that takes place along with the innovation process in interaction with business partners [Alegre *et al.*, 2011]. During the front-end phase of innovation process, external knowledge is detected and acquired. Thereafter, knowledge is assimilated to enable the decision-making regarding the potential innovation activities. During the concept creation phase external knowledge is combined with internal knowledge and finally, during the commercialization phase the new knowledge combinations are transformed into commercial ends. [cf. Cohen and Levinthal, 1990; Zahra and George, 2002.]

Although absorptive capacity has been closely linked with innovation success, it is a process that is difficult to measure and manage. Zahra and George [2002] and Branzei and Vertinsky [2006] have developed some indicators for measurement. The acquisition of knowledge can be measured based on the number of sources from which a firm obtains important knowledge for its innovation activities. In small firms, the typical sources of new knowledge are customers, suppliers and other non-competing partners. On the other hand, the direction and intensity in searching the different types of knowledge inputs for the innovation activities could be a potential indicator [Forsman, 2009a]. Correspondingly, the assimilation of knowledge can be measured by using a reflective question of to what extent a firm has incorporated these different knowledge inputs into its existing activities. [cf. Forsman and Temel, 2014.] Finally, the transformation of knowledge can be measured based on the output of innovation process. However, the innovative outputs and the fact how well these have been exploited in business will be discussed in relation to innovation performance element (Section 6.3.6).

The upper part of Table 6.5 summarizes the potential indicators for assessing the performance of external learning.

The internal learning process differs from the external one in that it is related to the accumulation of experiences inside a firm [Alegre *et al.*, 2011]. It is a process that increases shared knowledge among the staff members [Bierly and Hämäläinen, 1995]. Internal learning often starts with the creation of knowledge at individual level when for example an employee comes up with a new idea for improving products or processes [Kessler *et al.*, 2000]. Hence, individual creativity has an important role for stimulating the internal learning process [Bierly and Hämäläinen,

Table 6.5.   Indicators for managing the learning processes.

Indicators	Sources
External learning process	
The number and direction of sources from which a firm obtains external knowledge.	Branzei and Vertinsky [2006]
	Asheim [2007]
The intensity of using sources for obtaining external knowledge.	Forsman [2009a]
The extent to which a firm has incorporated external knowledge into its innovation activities.	Branzei and Vertinsky [2006]
The speed of incorporating the knowledge inputs into existing activities.	Zahra and George [2002]
Internal learning process	
The extent to which internal innovation landscape supports internal learning.	Starbuck [1992]
The extent to which the current practices stimulate internal learning process at individual level.	Kessler *et al.* [2000]
The extent to which the current practices promote knowledge diffusion.	Bierly and Hämäläinen [1995]
The volume and quality of immediate outcomes of internal learning.	Kessler *et al.* [2000]
Balance between internal and external learning processes	
How well the internal and external learning are in balance to strengthen and enlarge the knowledge base of a firm.	Bierly and Hämäläinen [1995]

1995]. Quite often these individuals introduce the idea first to their co-workers that belong to same community of practice sharing similar knowledge background [cf. Brown and Duguid, 1991]. For that reason, they can easily integrate new knowledge with existing one. However, this new knowledge is still an asset of this small community and it should be transformed in to firm-level knowledge. In small firms it does not need dramatic activities due to the small number of staff members but however, they should have some procedures for sharing new knowledge and transferring it to explicit one [cf. Nonaka and Takeuchi, 1995].

Based on prior literature Kessler *et al.* [2000] have summarized four characteristics in which internal learning can flourish. First, firm culture should support risk-taking, openness in communication and collaboration in order to give space for internal learning. Second, less-hierarchical structure makes knowledge diffusion easier. This quite often is the situation is small firms. Third, in order to be able to generate new knowledge through internal learning a critical mass of expertise is needed. In addition, such practices as cross-functional team work, job rotation, open communication channels and empowerment stimulate the internal learning process. Finally, if the external environment is too stable, it does not urge to learn. In such a situation there is no need to unlearn [Bierly and Hämäläinen, 1995]. On the other hand, if the environment is too turbulent, it inhibits the interpretation. Hence, internal learning seems to be at its best when the external environment is turbulent enough but not chaotic. This characteristic is, however, difficult to control by small firms. [Bierly and Hämäläinen, 1995; Kessler *et al.*, 2000.]

Hence, the internal learning process can be assessed based on perceptions of how well the internal innovation landscape supports internal learning, how established are the practices that support internal learning at individual level and the diffusion of this knowledge at firm-level. Finally, also the volume and quality of the immediate outcomes could be potential indicators (see Table 6.5).

Finally, internal and external learning are interrelated processes that complement each other. An adequate internal knowledge base is needed to be able to understand the value of external knowledge and exploit it to the specific needs of a firm [Cohen and Levinthal, 1990]. Thus, internal learning is a prerequisite for external learning. The internal learning process strengthens the own knowledge base of a firm and controllability of it while the external learning process is needed to enlarge this knowledge base [cf. Bierly and Hämäläinen, 1995; Kessler *et al.*, 2000]. Therefore, the internal and external learning processes should be in balance and this balance is one potential indicator to be assessed.

In summary, while both the internal and external learning processes are commonly identified to be the key factors to innovation success, they are challenging to measure due to their emergent and even unplanned nature. However, these processes stay on track and feed knowledge for innovation activities only when managed in a less-bureaucratic way in the favorable internal innovation landscape.

6.3.6 Innovation performance

While the previous chapters have focused on innovation efficiency answering the question of what is the degree of efforts made to achieve innovation success, this chapter focuses on the question of what is that degree of achieved innovation success. Hence, the innovation performance indicators measure how successfully the innovation potential has been transformed through innovation activities for creating value for the innovating firm and its stakeholders.

Commonly innovation performance has been measured based on the direct innovation outputs, for example by using the number of new product launches, new patents filings or the volume of new innovations. Some studies recommend also business success to be measured by using such indicators as growth in sales or percentage of sales in new products. However, firms should exploit their innovation potential in a way that they can efficiently deliver products and services to serve the expressed needs of their current customers while at the same time they should innovate to serve also the unexpressed needs of their current and potential new customers. On the other hand, the challenge with the business success indicators is that they demonstrate the results of past activities while these indicators are not predictive providing direction for the further innovation activities [Kaplan and Norton, 1996]. For that reason, Forsman [2008; 2009b] points out that innovation success should be measured not only based on innovation process output and business success but also on the basis of the impact on customer and future potentiality. This is in line with Shenhar *et al.* [2001] who have identified four success categories for projects: project efficiency, impact on customer, business success and preparing for the future. Table 6.6 presents a summary of indicators for these categories.

The first category, named in this chapter as innovation output, can be identified in a very short term by measuring after the completion of innovation activities the direct results of innovation activities, for example in terms of extension of product range and number of products phased out, number of new radical innovations and incremental improvements [OECD, 2005; CIS, 2010; Forsman and Annala, 2011].

On the other hand, the balance between incremental and radical innovations reflects the abilities of a firm to both exploration and exploitation.

Table 6.6.   Indicators for measuring innovation performance.

Indicators	Sources
Innovation output	
Number of new radical innovations	Forsman and Annala [2011]
Number of new incremental improvements	Forsman and Annala [2011]
Balance between radical and incremental outputs	March [1991]
	Raisch *et al.* [2009]
Extension of product range	OECD [2005]
Number of products phased out	OECD [2005]
Registered IPRs	Adams *et al.* [2006]
	Mendonca *et al.* [2004]
Impact on customer	
The extent to which the needs of customers are fulfilled	Shenhar *et al.* [2001]
Speed of customer adoption	Mankin [2007]
Changes in customer satisfaction	Shenhar *et al.* [2001]
Changes in customer loyalty	Mankin [2007]
Business success	
Value or percentage of sales from new innovation(s)	CIS [2010]
	Griffith *et al.* [2006]
Value or percentage of profits from new innovation(s)	CIS [2010]
Changes in internal efficiency	Shenhar *et al.* [2001]
Return on investment (ROI)	Mankin [2007]
Future potentiality	
Impact on knowledge base	Shenhar *et al.* [2001]
	Zahra and George [2002]
Opening of new markets	Alegre *et al.* [2009]
Impact on staff satisfaction	Kaplan and Norton [1996]
Impact on the reputation of a firm	Enzing *et al.* [2011]
	Shenhar *et al.* [2001]

As has been earlier discussed in this book, in small firms the exploration and exploitation activities compete for the same limited resources. Due to the uncertainty of returns from the exploration activities small firms may have tendency to increase the reliability of returns through the exploitation activities. Although this emphasis on the exploitation activities could result in higher short-term profits, it may also result in a competence trap [cf. March, 1991; Raisch *et al.*, 2009].

The patent filings are commonly used as an indicator for measuring technology-intensive innovations. This indicator ignores, however, the other types of intellectual assets that may be more important in small firms [cf. Adams *et al.*, 2006]. For example, Mendonca *et al.* [2004] point out that trademark filings can be used by a larger number of firms, also in the service businesses. According to them, a new trademark reflects the introduction of new offering(s) aimed at differentiating them from those provided by competitors. In addition, the other forms of registered IPRs, such as the designs and the utility models, can be included in IPR-related indicators. [cf. Forsman and Temel, 2014.]

The second category, impact on customer, emphasizes the importance placed on customer requirements and on fulfilling their needs. Customer impact can be assessed within the few months since a new offering is delivered to customers and they are using it. The appropriate indicators are related to customer satisfaction and customer loyalty measuring for example how well the product fulfills the needs of customers, how well the functionality fulfills the performance needs and how well the problems of customers are solved [Shenhar *et al.*, 2001; Mankin, 2007].

In order to measure the third category, business success, a longer time period is needed even from one to two years when a significant number of customer deliveries have been carried out. In the context of small business, the potential indicators for measuring business success are market-related and efficiency-related indicators, such as growth in sales, percentage of sales in new products, ROI, changes in relative and absolute profits and changes in the efficiency of internal processes [CIS, 2010; Alegre *et al.*, 2011; Forsman *et al.*, 2013].

While the above three categories have emphasis on the direct benefits gained through innovations, the future potentiality category tries to capture the benefits that will be realized indirectly in a longer period, probably after three to five years. Shenhar *et al.* [2001] advise to ask a question of how the developed innovations help a firm prepare for its future challenges.

The potential indicators for measuring future potentiality are such as impact on the knowledge base of a firm, opening of new markets, impact on staff satisfaction and the reputation of a firm. Positive values of these indicators will enhance the abilities of a firm to respond to external challenges and the unexpected actions of its competitors. [see for example Kaplan and Norton, 1996; Shenhar *et al.*, 2001; Alegre *et al.*, 2009; Forsman and Temel, 2014.]

In summary, these six sub-chapters have presented the elements of the innovation engine accompanied with potential indicators for measuring innovation in the context of small business. However, in order to take full advantage of this measurement, it must be utilized for managing the innovation activities of a firm. The next chapter focuses on this issue.

6.4 The Use of the Innovation Engine

As in today's turbulent business environment investments in innovation have become higher and higher also among small businesses, it is natural that firms seek to identify the ways how to measure and manage the impact of their innovation efforts. The critical questions are: what should be measured, what indicators should be used in measurement and how the measurement information should be used in decision making. Not any of these questions are easy to answer.

Regarding the question of what should be measured, the main advice is that the measurement dimensions should be derived from innovation goals. On the other hand, the innovation goals should be aligned with overall business goals. For example, if the business goal is to create better value for customers through innovation so as to gain improved ROI, then the factors related to this success should be measured in order to determine whether these goals have been achieved or not. However, while the measurement system should consider the strategic goals of a firm, also a strong focus should be on operational aspects, since they are critical for success in the context of small business [Garengo *et al.*, 2005].

On the other hand, in a situation where a firm tries to change significantly its directions, for example from incremental to radical innovations, it must also change the selection of performance metrics to focus less on the intended outcomes and more on the means by which these outcomes are to be achieved [Melnyk *et al.*, 2010]. Hence, in such a situation a great deal of attention should be shifted toward the question of how the new goals are to be attained. Two general challenges have been identified related to a situation in which firms change their directions. First, the firms have inadequate answers to the question of how the goals are to be accomplished and second, they fail to displace such behavior that is not anymore critical to success [Melnyk *et al.*, 2010]. Thus, dramatic changes demand not only efficient learning but also efficient unlearning.

In regard to the question of what indicators should be used in measurement in order to get full advantage of the indicators, they should be easy to implement and easy to use. In the context of small business, the clarity and simplicity of indicators are vital in importance for the successful implementation and use of them [cf. Janssen *et al.*, 2011; Garengo *et al.*, 2005]. What comes to the number of indicators, the optimal set of indicators varies from firm to firm. For example, innovation for a furniture manufacturer will require different resources, capabilities and equipment than innovation for a game developer. Nevertheless, the typical challenges in measuring are not the lack of indicators but the fact that too many indicators are used in measurement. In addition, the indicators are all too often exclusively the outcome-based lagging indicators that cannot explain what drives innovation [Kuczmarski, 2001].

Sometimes indicators are misleading directing firms towards undesired outcomes. Small firms should be aware of unintended consequences as a result of over-emphasizing one single indicator. Melnyk *et al.* [2010] present an example of a misleading indicator in which a firm used percentage of sales from new products as an indicator for measuring performance. While this indicator demonstrated high values, they were, however, achieved by dropping out the older products that still had potential. On the contrary, the new products that should have been abandoned were kept on the list.

What is clear is that no single indicator can exhibit in isolation the full meaning of performance. In order to get a comprehensive view of innovation performance in a firm, it is needed to have a set of indicators. Muller *et al.* [2005] argue that the optimal number of indicators is 10 or below while Andrew *et al.* [2010] point out that 10 to 12 indicators are needed to provide such information that is required to manage instead of just reacting. The majority of firms seem to use five or even a smaller number of indicators. According to Andrew *et al.* [2010], it is not adequate for specifying the goals of innovation and for identifying the challenges that may hinder the progress towards these goals. However, it seems that developing indicators is easier than killing them. Kuczmarski [2001] highlights that when the indicators are not anymore relevant, firms should let the current indicators go.

In the context of small business, it would be better to use a few vital indicators and communicate them in a visually effective way, for example as graphs [Cocca and Alberti, 2010]. This book recommends that small firms build a set of indicators covering all six elements of the innovation engine. With a comprehensive set of indicators, small firms will more probably identify the dormant challenges in their innovation activities helping them make the right decisions resulting in a higher innovation success.

Nevertheless, it is recommended to avoid a tendency to measure everything. It could lead to a non-manageable set of indictors, over-load of data and high measurement costs. As Neely [2004] states, it is not that the wrong things are measured but too much is measured. On the other hand, Hempel [2006] points out that the management needs a different set of indicators than do the employees that are executing the innovation goals.

Regarding the question of how measurement information should be used in decision making, it may be more challenging to use the measurement information than to design the indicators for measurement. For example, Kuczmarski [2001] identified that despite the existence of indicators, the measurement practices are infrequent. It is clear that the procedures to collect data should be put in place. In addition, it is needed to establish a forum to review the data and agree the actions. In order to do this, a regular meeting is needed [Bourne *et al.*, 2000]. These meetings should be held for example on a monthly basis [cf. Hudson *et al.*, 2001]. In a firm with open communication culture and empowerment, the participants should include both the managers and the employees.

In small firms the financial and computer systems may not be sophisticated enough for providing complicated measurement information on a regular basis. For that reason, small firms should consider what kind of information is easily accessible or could even be manually calculated. Based on the information that is available, the indicators should be selected. Nevertheless, it is needed to avoid such a situation in which the expenses of collecting measurement information are higher than the benefits of using it in decision making.

The resistance to measurement has been identified as one challenge in small firms [Hudson Smith and Smith, 2007]. It can inhibit the implementation and use of measurement systems. The staff members may resist the efforts allocated to data collection for which they cannot see any use [Hudson *et al.*, 2001]. This is very likely if the staff members have not been involved in designing the system and its indicators. A beneficial solution could be that measurement information is available to all staff members and updated on a regular basis. Especially if the measurement information can be presented in one or two graphs, the visibility of them could increase the commitment of employees to the actions needed to be taken. Nevertheless, the high visibility of measurement results and required actions accompanied with open communication may decrease this resistance.

One would expect that when a firm has designed a measurement framework, implemented the appropriate indicators and started to use this system for managing innovation, a firm is at the destination. No, it is not there, the journey should continue. Due to the fact that small firms operate in a highly dynamic environment in which it is needed to continually adapt to market changes, these changes should be quickly reflected in their system for measuring and managing performance [Cocca and Alberti, 2010]. For that reason, it would be a worthwhile idea to assess also the system itself and how well it fulfills the main criteria for efficient and reliable performance measurement and management of it. This can be done for example by discussing the following questions: how well the system directs innovation activities, whether performance indicators are relevant providing fast and accurate feedback, does the system provide contribution for monitoring the past performance as well as for planning the future performance, whether all stakeholders are considered and finally, does the system stimulate continuous learning and improvement [Hudson *et al.*, 2001; Cocca and Alberti, 2010]. Measuring innovation is a continuous process that needs to be updated with changing conditions.

6.5 Chapter Summary

The aim of this chapter was to discuss how small firms improve their competitiveness and chances for business success by measuring innovation. Prior literature has shown that there exists a deep gap between the goals of innovation and the returns of it. Inadequate or even missing measurement practices have been proposed as one reason for this. However, measurement has both supporters as well as opponents. The supporters refer to an old phrase *"You cannot manage what you do not measure"* while the opponents explain that measurement as a tool for command and control smothers innovativeness in organizations.

Hence, it can be assumed that despite the size of the firm, there will always emerge some degree of resistance towards measurement. This resistance can be overcome by open communication and discussion about the advantages and disadvantages of measurement. Without a shared understanding on the needs of measurement, implementing such a system could be a mission impossible.

Directing decision making is a commonly presented advantage of measurement. However, in the context of small business, the main goal of measurement should be learning. Hence, the measurement of innovation should help small firms learn to perform well. The disadvantages of measurement are commonly related to increased bureaucracy and the expenses of data collection and analysis.

In small firms the measurement practices seem to be *ad hoc* or even missing due to their limited managerial capacity, short-term strategic planning, lack of resources and reactive or even disinclined approach to measurement. On the other hand, it has been explained that they do not need measurement because all problems are visible and people get to know them without having such systems. This has been found to be true in a situation where a firm is running its businesses in a stable environment with emphasis on local markets. However, competition is tightening also in the local markets and small firms are facing a more unpredictable change. The more turbulent and volatile the business environment is, the more necessary is comprehensive performance measurement.

In this chapter the measurement challenges were approached based on three questions: what should be measured, what indicators should be used in measurement and how the measurement information should be utilized in decision making. None of these questions has an easy answer.

The first two questions were answered by presenting a system-based innovation engine that helps small firms innovate and learn. The aim of the innovation engine is to demonstrate innovation performance, not only based on the past success of innovation activities but also outlining the potential future success of these activities. In the best scenario, the use of this system should lead to a self-reinforcing innovation-learning cycle in which the reflection of innovation activities results in learning which in turn leads to the identification of even more challenging innovation goals. The implementation of these new goals will through reflection lead to a new level of learning.

The innovation engine consists of six elements: external innovation landscape, internal innovation landscape, innovation potential, innovation process and activities, internal and external learning processes and finally, innovation performance.

Innovation is a contextual phenomenon and the context as an innovation landscape either encourages or hampers innovation. The first two elements assess how well the external and internal environments support innovation in small firms. Regarding the external innovation landscape, small firms have limited abilities to control it. Instead, they should be aware of opportunities it offers. In addition, they should assess the functionality of this environment, and this is an issue also small firms can influence. Finally, innovation is not anymore the domain of one firm. Hence, one important aspect is to monitor the diversity and structure of external business partners that can significantly enhance the innovation potential of small firms.

While small firms have limited abilities to influence their external innovation landscape, they can create a favorable ground for internal innovation activities. The common characteristics of fertile internal innovation landscape are the intention to be innovative, the procedures that support innovativeness in a firm accompanied with innovation and market-oriented culture and behavior.

The third element, innovation potential, includes tangible and intangible resources allocated to innovation activities while the fourth element, innovation process and activities, is interested in how this potential is transformed into innovation performance. The innovation potential consists of such items as financial resources, human resources, equipment and facilities. Correspondingly, the innovation process and activities that make use of these resources are measured based on the quality of process and activities.

The innovation studies unanimously emphasize the vital role of learning and knowledge-related processes for innovation success, especially if the firms are operating in the highly dynamic environments. In the innovation engine, the fifth element, learning, was approached from two aspects, internal learning and external learning. While internal learning improves knowledge and capabilities by using the internal resources and experiences of a firm, external learning creates new knowledge through interaction with external partners. However, these two learning processes complement each other. The internal learning process strengthens the firm's own knowledge base while the external learning process is needed to enlarge this knowledge base to the specific areas. Therefore, the internal and external learning processes should be in balance.

The sixth element of the innovation engine, innovation performance, focuses on the degree of innovation success. Thus, innovation performance reflects how successfully innovation potential has been transformed through innovation activities for creating value for the innovating firm and its stakeholders. Four success categories focusing on the different aspects and time frames of performance are identified: innovation output, impact on customer, impact on business and future potentiality.

Innovation output demonstrates the direct results of innovation activities such as new innovations and processes while the impact on customers reflects how satisfied the customers are with these innovations. Innovation output can be measured immediately after the completion of innovation tasks. Instead, the impact on customers can be measured for a few months since offerings are delivered to customers and they are in use.

Impact on business demonstrates how well a firm has managed in commercialization and value appropriation. For measuring impact on business, a longer time span is needed, even from one to two years when a significant number of customer deliveries have been carried out. Finally, future potentiality tries to capture the benefits that will be realized indirectly after a longer period of time. A key question for assessing it is how the innovations help a firm prepare for its future challenges.

While the innovation engine helps small firms measure their innovation activities, it also allows management to see performance across a variety of innovation facets. It provides a framework against which small business owner-managers can assess the extent and quality of their own innovation activities and identify the potential areas for improvements. In addition to learning, it is believed that the innovation engine will help small firms unlearning from the current practices and giving space for the new ones. They both are needed in the circumstances of continuous and rapid change.

Innovation measurement accompanied by benchmarking the innovation activities is especially recommended for such firms that aim to change significantly their directions. In such situations, in addition to defining strategic goals, a great deal of attention should be addressed to the question of how the new goals are to be attained. Hence, a strong focus should be on operational aspects, since they are critical for success in small firms in transition.

References

Adams, R., Bessant, J. and Phelps, R. (2006). Innovation management measurement: A review, *International Journal of Management Reviews*, 8(1), pp. 21–47.

Alegre, J., Chiva, R. and Lapiedra, R. (2009). Measuring innovation in long product development cycle industries: An insight in biotechnology, *Technology Analysis & Strategic Management*, 21(4), pp. 535–546.

Alegre, J., Sengupta, K. and Lapiedra, R. (2011). Knowledge management and innovation performance in a high-tech SMEs industry, *International Small Business Journal*, 31(4), pp. 454–470.

Amabile, T.M. (1998). How to kill creativity, *Harvard Business Review*, 76(5), pp. 77–87.

Anderson, N.R. and West, M.A. (1998). Measuring climate for work group innovation: Development and validation of the team climate inventory, *Journal of Organizational Behavior*, 19, pp. 235–258.

Andrew, J.P., Manget, J., Michael, D.C., Taylor, A. and Zablit, H. (2010). *Innovation 2010. A return to prominence — and the emergence of a new world order.* Report. (Boston Consulting Group, Boston).

Asheim, B. (2007). Differentiated knowledge bases and varieties of regional innovation systems, *The European Journal of Social Science Research*, 20(3), pp. 223–241.

Ateljevic, J. and Doorne, S. (2004). Diseconomies of scale: A study of development constraints in small tourism firms in central New Zealand, *Tourism and Hospitality Research*, 5(1), pp. 5–24.

Aubert, J.E. (2005). *Promoting Innovation in Developing Countries: A Conceptual Framework*. World Bank Policy Research Working Papers 3554. Online. Available at: http://econ.worldbank.org (Accessed 16.04.2014).

Bessant, J. (2003). *High Involvement Innovation: Building and Sustaining Competitive Advantage through Continuous Change*. (John Wiley, Chichester).

Bierly, P.B. and Hämäläinen, T. (1995). Organizational learning and strategy, *Scandinavian Journal of Management*, 11(3), pp. 209–224.

Birchall, D., Tovstiga, G. and Gaule, A. (2004). *Innovation Performance Measurement, Striking the Right Balance*. (Grist Ltd, London).

Birchall, D., Chanaron, J-J., Tovstiga, G. and Hillenbrand, C. (2011). Innovation performance measurement: Current practices, issues and management challenges, *International Journal of Technology Management*, 56(1), pp. 1–20.

Bititci, U.S., Mendibil, K., Nudurupati, S., Garengo, P. and Turner, T. (2006). Dynamics of Performance measurement and organizational culture, *International Journal of Operations and Production Management*, 26(12), pp. 1325–1350.

Bititci, U., Garengo, P., Dörfler, V. and Nudupurati, S. (2012). Performance measurement: Challenges for tomorrow, *International Journal of Management Reviews*, 14(3), pp. 305–327.

Branzei, O. and Vertinsky, I. (2006). Strategic pathways to product innovation capabilities in SMEs, *Journal of Business Venturing*, 21(1), pp. 75–105.

Bourne, M., Mills, J., Wilcox, M., Neely, A. and Platts, K. (2000). Designing, implementing and updating performance measurement systems, *International Journal of Operations & Production Management*, 20(7), pp. 754–771.

Brown, J.S. and Duguid, P. (1991). Organizational learning and communities-in-practice: Toward a unified view of working, learning and innovation, *Organization Science*, 2(1), pp. 40–57.

Brown, M.G., and Svenson, R.A. (1998). Measuring R&D productivity, *Research Technology Management*, 41(6), pp. 11–15.

Cainelli, G., Evangelista, R. and Savona, M. (2006). Innovation and economic performance in services: A firm-level analysis, *Cambridge Journal of Economics*, 30(3), pp. 435–458.

Cedergren, S., Wall, A. and Norström, C. (2010). Evaluation of performance in a product development context, *Business Horizons*, 53(4), pp. 359–369.

Christopherson, S. and Clark, J. (2007). Power in firm networks: What it means for regional innovation systems, *Regional Studies*, 41(9), pp. 1223–1236.

Cooke, P., Clifton, N. and Oleaga, M. (2005). Social capital, firm embeddedness and regional development, *Regional Studies*, 39(8), pp. 1065–1077.

CIS (2010). *Community Innovation Survey*, 2010. (Eurostat: European Commission). Online. Available at: http://ec.europa.eu/eurostat (Accessed 14.02.2015).

Cocca, P. and Alberti, M. (2010). A framework to assess performance measurement systems in SMEs, *International Journal of Productivity and Performance Management*, 59(2), pp. 186–200.

Cohen, W.M. and Levinthal, D.A. (1990). Absorptive capacity: A new perspective on learning and innovation, *Administrative Science Quarterly*, 35(1), pp. 128–152.

Cooper, R.G., Edgett, S.J. and Kleinschmidt, E.J. (1999). New product portfolio management: Practices and performance, *Journal of Product Innovation Management*, 16(4), pp. 333–351.

Damanpour, F. (1992). Organizational size and innovation, *Organizational Studies*, 13(3), pp. 375–402.

Damanpour, F. and Gopalakrishnan, S. (2001). The dynamics of the adoption of product and process innovations in organizations, *Journal of Management Studies*, 38(1), pp. 45–65.

Davenport, T.H. (2006). Competing on analytics, *Harvard Business Review*, 84(1), pp. 98–107.

Davila, T., Epstein M.J. and Shelton R.D. (2012). *Making Innovation Work: How to Manage It, Measure It, and Profit from It.* (Pearson Education, Upper Saddle River, New Jersey).

Dobni, C.B. (2008). Measuring innovation culture in organizations: The development of a generalized innovation culture construct using exploratory factor analysis, *European Journal of Innovation Management*, 11(4), pp. 539–559.

Enzing, C.M., Battering, M.H., Janszen, F.H.A. and Omta, S.W.F (2011). Where innovation processes make a difference in products' short- and long-term market success, *British Food Journal*, 113(7), pp. 812–837.

Flor, M.L. and Oltra, M.J. (2004). Identification of innovating firms through technological innovation indicators: An application to the Spanish ceramic tile industry, *Research Policy*, 33(2), pp. 323–336.

Forsman, H. (2008). Business development success in SMEs: A case study approach, *Journal of Small Business and Enterprise Development*, 15(3), pp. 606–622.

Forsman, H. (2009a). Balancing capability building for radical and incremental innovations, *International Journal of Innovation Management*, 13(4), pp. 501–520.

Forsman, H. (2009b). Improving innovation capabilities of small enterprises: Cluster strategy as a tool, *International Journal of Innovation Management*, 13(2), pp. 221–243.

Forsman, H. (2011). Innovation capacity and innovation development in small enterprises. A comparison between the manufacturing and service sectors, *Research Policy*, 40(5), pp. 739–750.

Forsman, H. and Annala, U. (2011). Small enterprises as innovators: Shift from a low performer to a high performer, *International Journal of Technology Management*, 56(2/3/4), pp. 154–171.

Forsman, H. and Temel, S. (2014). Measuring for Innovation, in eds. Gupta, P. and Trusko, B., *Global Innovation Science Handbook*. (McGraw-Hill, New York, USA).

Forsman, H., Temel, S. and Uotila, M. (2013). Towards sustainable competitiveness: Comparison of the successful and unsuccessful eco-innovators, *International Journal of Innovation Management*, 17(3).

Freel, M.S. and Harrison, R.T. (2006). Innovation and cooperation in the small firm sector: Evidence from Northern Britain, *Regional Studies*, 40(4), pp. 289–305.

Galindo, A.J. and Micco, A. (2007). Creditor protection and credit response to shocks, *The World Bank Economic Review*, 21(3), pp. 413–438.

Garengo, P., Biazzo, S. and Bititci, U.S. (2005). Performance measurement systems in SMEs: A review for a research agenda, *International Journal of Management Reviews*, 7(1), pp. 25–47.

Griffith, R., Huergo, E., Mairesse, J. and Peters, B. (2006). Innovation and productivity across four European countries, *Oxford Review of Economic Policy*, 22(4), pp. 483–498.

Hempel, J. (2006). Metrics madness. Quantifying innovation is key. Here's how to do it right and avoid the big mistakes managers often make, *Business Week*, 25 September, pp. 34–35.

Hudson, M., Smart, A. and Bourne, M. (2001). Theory and practice in SME performance measurement systems, *International Journal of Operations & Production Management*, 21(8), pp. 1096–1115.

Hudson Smith, M. and Smith, D. (2007). Implementing strategically aligned performance measurement in small firms, *International Journal of Production Economies*, 106(2), pp. 393–408.

Janssen, S., Moeller, K. and Schlaefke, M. (2011). Using performance measures conceptually in innovation control, *Journal of Management Control*, 22(1), pp. 107–128.

Jarvis, R., Curran, J., Kitching, J. and Lightfoot, G. (2000). The use of quantitative and qualitative criteria in the measurement of performance in small firms, *Journal of Small Business and Enterprise Development*, 7(2), pp. 123–134.

Kaplan, R.S. and Norton, D.P. (1996). Using the balanced scorecard as a strategic management system, *Harvard Business Review*, 74(1), pp. 75–85.

Kang, K.N. and Lee, Y.S. (2008). What affects the innovation performance of small and medium-sized enterprises (SMEs) in the biotechnology industry? An empirical study on Korean biotech SMEs, *Biotechnology Letters*, 30(10), pp. 1699–1704.

Kessler, E.H., Bierly, P.E. and Gopalakrishnan, S. (2000). Internal vs. External learning in new product development: Effects on speed, costs and competitive advantage, *R&D Management*, 30(3), pp. 213–223.

Kessler, E.H. and Chakrabarti, A.K. (1996). Innovation speed: A conceptual model of context, antecedents, and outcomes, *The Academy of Management Review*, 21(4), pp. 1143–1191.

Kuczmarski, T.D. (2001). Five fatal flaws of innovation metrics, *Marketing Management*, 10(1), pp. 34–39.

Laitinen, E.K. (2002). A dynamic performance measurement system: Evidence from small Finnish technology companies, *Scandinavian Journal of Management*, 18(1), pp. 65–99.

Lin, C.Y.-Y. and Zhang, J. (2005). Changing structures of SME networks: Lessons from the publishing industry in Taiwan, *Long Range Planning*, 38(2), pp. 145–162.

Mankin, E. (2007). Measuring innovation performance, *Research Technology Management*, 50(6), pp. 5–7.

March, J.G. (1991). Exploration and exploitation in organizational learning, *Organization Science*, 2(1), pp. 71–87.

Mazzarol, T. and Reboud, S. (2008). The role of complementary actors in the development of innovation in small firms, *International Journal of Innovation Management*, 12(2), pp. 223–253.

Melnyk, S.A., Hanson, J.D. and Calantone, R.J. (2010). Hitting the target … but missing the point: Resolving the paradox of strategic transition, *Long Range Planning*, 43(4), pp. 555–574.

Mendonca, S., Pereira, T.S. and Godinho, M.M. (2004). Trademarks as an indicator of innovation and industrial change, *Research Policy*, 33(9), pp. 1385–1404.

Molleman, E. and Timmerman, H. (2003). Performance management when innovation and learning become critical performance indicators, *Personnel Review*, 32(1), pp. 93–113.

Muller, A., Välikangas, L. and Merlyn, P. (2005). Metrics for innovation: Guidelines for developing a customized suite of innovation metrics, *Strategy & Leadership*, 33(1), pp. 37–45.

Neely, A. (2004). Performance measurement: The new crisis, in eds. Crainer, S. and Dearlove, D., *Financial Times Handbook of Management*. (Pearson Education Ltd, Harlow).

Nieto, M.J. and Santamaria, L. (2007). The importance of diverse collaborative networks for the novelty of product innovation, *Technovation*, 27(6–7), pp. 367–377.

Nonaka, I. and Takeuchi, H. (1995). *The Knowledge-Creating Company*. (Oxford University Press: New York).

OECD (2005). *Oslo Manual. Guidelines for Collecting and Interpreting Innovation Data*. (A joint publication of OECD and Eurostat). Online. Available at: www.oecd.org. (Accessed 16.06.2014).

Pedersen, E.R.G. and Sudzina, F. (2012). Which firms use measures? Internal and external factors shaping the adoption of performance measurement systems in Danish firms, *International Journal of Operations & Production Management*, 32(1), pp. 4–27.

Prashantham, S. and Birkinshaw, J. (2008). Dancing with Gorillas: How small companies can partner effectively with MNCs, *California Management Review*, 51(1), pp. 6–23.

Raisch, S., Birkinshaw, J., Probst, G. and Tushman, M.L. (2009). Organizational ambidexterity: Balancing exploitation and exploration for sustained performance, *Organization Science*, 20(4), pp. 685–695.

Rammer, C., Czarnitzki, D. and Spielkamp, A. (2009). Innovation success of non-R&D-performers: Substituting technology by management in SMEs, *Small Business Economics*, 33(1), pp. 35–58.

Robson, P.J.A. and Obeng, B.A. (2008). The barriers to growth in Ghana, *Small Business Economics*, 30(4), pp. 385–403.

Rowley, T., Behrens, D. and Krackhardt, D. (2000). Redundant governance structures: An analysis of structural and relational embeddedness in the steel and semiconductor industries, *Strategic Management Journal*, 21(3), pp. 369–386.

Shane, S., Venkataraman, S. and MacMillan, I. (1995). Cultural differences in innovation championing strategies, *Journal of Management*, 21(5), pp. 931–952.

Shenhar, A.J., Dvir, D., Levy, O. and Maltz, A.C. (2001), Project success: A multidimensional strategic concept, *Long Range Planning*, 34(6), pp. 699–725.

Simpson, M., Padmore, J. and Newman, N. (2012). Towards a new model of success and performance in SMEs, *International Journal of Entrepreneurial Behaviour & Research*, 18(3), 264–285.

Starbuck, W.H. (1992). Learning by knowledge-intensive firms, *Journal of Management Studies*, 29(6), pp. 713–740.

Subramanian, A. and Nilakanta, S. (1996). Organizational innovativeness: Exploring the relationship between organizational determinants of innovation, types of innovations, and measures of organizational performance, *Omega*, 24(6), pp. 631–647.

Tran, T. (2008). A conceptual model of learning culture and innovation schema, *Competitiveness Review: An International Business Journal*, 18(3), pp. 287–299.

Zahra, S.A. and George, G. (2002). Absorptive capacity: A review, reconceptualization, and extension, *Academy of Management Review*, 27(2), pp. 185–203.

Zollo, M. and Winter, S.G. (2002). Deliberate learning and the evolution of dynamic capabilities, *Organization Science*, 13(3), pp. 339–351.

Chapter 7

Conclusions for Moving Forward

7.1 Introduction

Despite the vital importance of small firms to the economies, our knowledge of the processes and dynamics of how small firms innovate, compete and grow is still very fragmented and even scant. The aim of this book was to contribute to this gap.

By taking the readers on a journey across the spectrum of small firms as innovators, the aim was to answer the question of how to strengthen innovation in small firms helping them grow and prosper. The journey started by exploring the innovation activities of small firms resulting in the identification of four divergent innovators: Low Performers, Incremental Performers, Radical Performers and High Performers.

The journey continued together with these innovators by exploring how the innovation capacity of these four profiles differs from each other and how this capacity changes on the way from a non-innovator to a high innovation performer. Thereafter, the readers were taken on the ride of creating competitiveness and growth in small firms. The accumulation of experiences obtained along this journey led to us to design an innovation engine to small firms for learning how to grow.

Along with this journey, it became evident that the High Performers possess the best abilities to grow and prosper. For that reason, these concluding marks are provided by echoing their characteristics, activities and

185

processes as a potential basis for success. Therefore, the High Performers are compared against the typical small firms. In addition, recommendations are presented for filling the gap between these two types of small firms. In order to provide the basis for benchmarking, the characteristics of the High Performer are summarized first.

As mentioned above, the High Performer seems to have the best abilities to succeed, not only during the favorable economic situation but also during the recession. It possesses a high capacity to innovate and its capabilities are in balance for both the exploration and exploitation activities. This demonstrates that this firm is capable to exploit today's business opportunities as well as to explore tomorrow's opportunities. The High Performer is a continuous innovator characterized by a proactive approach to changes, the highly diversified innovation activities and the strong innovation management practices. The innovation behavior and characteristics of this firm indicate that it has focus on fulfilling the expressed needs of their current customers as well as on exploring the unexpressed needs of potential future customers. The diversified innovation activities and proactive innovative behavior enable the High Performer to maintain its competitive trend.

Hence, if one wants to locate the firms that are more likely growing in terms of market-related, efficiency-related and employment-related indicators, it would be better to search them among the High Performers. These firms accommodate a high share of super growers, high growers and job creators. The super growers are growing sustainably in several fronts, the high growers have periods of very high growth and the job creators are continuously providing new job opportunities.

Based on the empirical evidence of this book, the above combination of characteristics, processes and activities can be considered as a success recipe of small firms for sustainable competitiveness and growth. However, only the minority of small firms follow the above success recipe. Instead, the vast majority of them are occasional innovators with low innovation diversity, poor or non-existent innovation management practices and they are inclined to react to the changes in their business environment by making incremental improvements in their current products and services. In the following comparison the archetype of this group of firms is named as "*a typical firm*". Let us take a look at the characteristics of this firm.

The typical firm has adopted a pure cost-efficiency strategy having a focus on efficiency-related performance and efficient internal processes resulting in a moderate profit level. Despite its profits, this firm allocates relatively low resources to the formal RD activities while its abilities for hidden innovation are better. The reactive innovation behavior and minimal efforts given to the innovation activities are entailing a risk of losing its competitiveness in the future. While the current innovation capabilities of the typical firm are relatively low, it has identified a need for developing such capabilities that will improve its abilities to respond to the future business opportunities. However, taking such a step demands substantial investments in capacity renovation accompanied by a risk of sacrificing its current profit level. Nevertheless, risk propensity and the risk management capabilities in the typical firm tend to be too poor for implementing this kind of strategy.

Hence, it can be summarized that a typical firm has potential to be more successful. An important question is how this firm can be encouraged to take such steps that will bring it closer to the success recipe. In this comparison the attempt will be made by using the innovation engine as a framework for comparing these two different kinds of innovators, *"the High Performer"* and *"the typical firm"*. Let us start from the external innovation landscape.

7.2 Influencing the External Innovation Landscape

While the High Performer as a proactive firm is aware of the changes in its external environment, the typical firm does not track the potential opportunities and threats of its business environment. Instead, the typical firm is trying to react to changes when they occur. In addition, while the High Performer tries to influence the functionality of its regional business environment, the typical firm takes the degree of functionality as cut and dried. Finally, by collaborating the resource-scarce small firms can improve significantly their capacity to innovate. While the typical firm collaborates especially in operative issues, the High Performer has a balanced structure in its partner network enabling it to benefit along with the innovation process covering both the innovation development activities as well as the commercialization activities.

In order to fill the gap between the High Performer and the typical small firm, the innovation engine recommends that the typical firm should establish some light practices to systematically monitor and analyze the changes in its business environment. In addition, the innovation engine recommends that the typical firm should assess how well the business environment satisfies the needs of it and its employees. This satisfaction should also be passed on to the associations dedicated to represent industries and entrepreneurs in policy-making. While the typical firm has limited (or even nonexistent) control over its external environment, it could, however, influence the functionality of its business environment.

Finally, as mentioned above, the innovation capacity of small firms can be enhanced through collaboration. For that reason, the external innovation landscape should be assessed in the light of opportunities it provides for obtaining external resources through partnering. The innovation engine recommends that the typical firm should take the first step by evaluating the structure of its current partners and the activities it serves. Along with the diversification of activities this structure should be strengthened and balanced to cover the critical activities in which collaboration provides advantages. However, the typical firm should be critical since collaboration can also lead to disadvantages in terms of higher expenses, the complex coordination of collaborative efforts and the lost control over the resources.

Regarding the external innovation landscape, one challenge that is relevant to all small firms emerges from empirical evidence used in this book. It is the low usage of regional development and consulting services provided by the development agencies, research organizations and educational institutes. However, this is a message to policy-makers directing the development and supply of these services. The low usage reflects that these services do not meet the needs of small firms. In addition, it seems that there exists a cognitive gap between the service providers and small firms. One reason for this could be the fact that commonly the policy-makers have been interested in young technology-oriented firms as potential high-growth firms and the regional services have been designed for their needs. Hence, it should be acknowledged that the high growers can emerge from all industries, and also among the established firms. On the other hand, the needs of the other types of growers, such as sustainable growers, job growers and hidden champions should also be explored when these services are designed.

In summary, while small firms have a limited power to control the external innovation landscape, they have a full power to design a fertile internal landscape to support innovation. Let us move on and step into the internal innovation landscape.

7.3 Towards a Fertile Internal Innovation Landscape

The innovation engine recommends that in order to provide a fertile ground for innovation, the internal landscape should include innovation and market-oriented behavior and culture, the intention to be innovative and the procedures should be in place to support innovativeness in a firm.

The High Performer possesses a medium-term vision for its business and based on this vision, it has identified the future goals. These goals direct to select the innovation activities. Instead, the typical firm has not defined its innovation goals and it is running its business directed by a short-term vision.

While the owner-manager of the High Performer has a significant and visible role in goal setting and decision making, the employees can participate in it especially regarding the issues that are related to their own work. Instead, in the typical firm decision making is in the hands of one individual, the owner-manager, who loves to focus on the operational activities, not on envisioning and strategic thinking. While this individual communicates efficiently with its employees, he or she is not willing to share his/her power to make decisions.

Finally, along with the diversified innovation activities, the High Performer has established a wide range of innovation management practices to support the activities for achieving the innovation goals. Instead, the typical firm does not have the clear goals for innovation and it possesses quite poor innovation management practices.

In order to fill the above gap, the innovation engine suggests that the typical firm should focus first on its innovation behavior and culture. It can be started by answering some qualitative questions, for example, how much the owner-manager spends his or her time on innovation and whether the employees are supported to present new ideas. In order to influence culture the best ways to do it are reflection, communication and collaboration.

In the next step it would be useful to focus on the strength of the intention of being innovative. The main question is whether the typical firm has defined the goals for innovation. If not, it should start by crystallizing its business goals. The innovation goals should be derived from them.

Finally, the typical firm should start establishing the innovation management practices to support innovation. However, due to the fact that in small firms this should be integrated in learning and learning takes place as a byproduct of innovation activities, the first step is to become aware of the need of some formal procedures. Thereafter, it would be better to start establishing the appropriate practices and procedures for the current activities and continue this along with the process of diversifying activities.

However, these new activities need new innovation potential. Let us move on to explore the potential of these small firms to innovate.

7.4 Enhancing Innovation Potential

Innovation potential consists of innovation enablers that can be tangible and intangible resources to be allocated to innovation activities. It is natural that the High Performer with its established innovation management practices has also the formal activities for innovation development. It allocates from two to three per cent of its sales to these activities. In addition, due to its wealthy track records, the abilities of the High Performer to support also hidden innovation are very good. Instead, the typical firm does not have the innovation management practices or the formal RD activities in place, and for that reason the value of resources allocated to the development work is very low. However, its abilities for hidden innovation are much better.

Regarding the human resources, the High Performer possesses high innovation capabilities. In addition, it possesses high prior abilities to develop innovations as well as to successfully commercialize them. Through its diversified partner network the High Performer gathers a rich diversity of relevant new ideas for its innovation activities. On the contrary, the typical firm possesses much weaker capabilities to innovate.

In addition, its capabilities are biased towards exploiting the current business opportunities instead of exploring the future opportunities. Hence, while the typical firm possesses quite high abilities to develop innovations, its prior abilities to commercialize these innovations are much weaker. In addition, the typical firm has emphasis on gathering ideas for improving its current products and services while it ignores gathering ideas for preparing to future business.

Hence, there seems to be a gap between the High Performer and the typical firm. In such a situation, the innovation engine directs to monitor the innovation potential divided into five aspects: financial resources, human resources, capture and generation of new ideas, external resources and the equipment and facilities.

It would be useful for the typical firm to start analyzing what kinds of resources are needed to achieve its innovation goals and try to find the optimal balance between the resources and the goals. In order to improve its human resources and idea generation, this can be started by collaborating more efficiently with the existing partner network. The typical firm possesses adequate abilities to exploit the current business opportunities. However, it is evident that the radical improvements in human resources are required if the typical firm aims to change its directions significantly. This demands serious efforts allocated to creating new knowledge and fostering the learning processes. What comes to the formal RD activities, the typical firm should on the basis of its innovation goals consider the needed allocations especially for exploring the future opportunities.

While innovation potential affects success, even more important for achieving success is the efficiency of the process for transforming this potential into innovation performance. Let us move on to monitor this process.

7.5 Speeding Up the Innovation Process

The innovation process and activities transform innovation potential into exploitable innovation outputs and business success. The critical issues are the progress and speed of the process and efficient communication to support them.

When assessing the quality of innovation processes and activities of the High Performer, it is evident that its sophisticated innovation management practices provide a cutting edge to be successful. In addition, through its diversified innovation activities the High Performer has learnt to facilitate efficiently innovation activities. Instead, the typical firm has less diversified innovation activities and thus, its prior experiences for facilitating these activities are weaker and narrower. However, as mentioned earlier, the typical firm possesses high abilities for improving its current products, services and processes. The challenges will emerge when it intends to shift to developing new innovations that demand a clear departure from the past activities.

For this situation, the innovation engine recommends that the typical firm should monitor the quality of innovation process and its activities. In addition, it is needed that the typical firm improves its abilities to adopt new ideas and inventions generated by others. Also regarding these adoptions, the rate and speed of adoption are the important indicators. Due to the fact that the typical firm has an imbalance between the innovation efforts for enhancing existing business and exploring new business, it would be useful to start step by step to balance them. This means that there should be a balance between the incremental and radical activities as well as between the high-risk and low-risk innovation efforts. Finally, the typical firm should increase its risk propensity by improving the capabilities to manage the risks.

While improving the quality of innovation processes and activities may help the typical firm improve its abilities to achieve business success, the learning process is in a vital role for sustaining this success. Hence, let us take a look at the learning process.

7.6 Learning to Innovate, Compete and Grow

The innovation engine framework highlights the two-folded relationship between learning and innovation. The innovation activities provide opportunities for learning by doing which in turn, improves the capabilities of a firm to innovate. The faster the firm learns, the faster it succeeds through innovation.

The High Performer through its diversified innovation activities has a rich diversity of learning opportunities. On the other hand, its ambitious innovation goals drive and foster its internal learning process and the accumulation of experiences. Instead, due to its less-ambitious innovation goals and one-sided innovation activities, the typical firm has a much poorer environment to foster the internal learning process. In addition, due to the lack of formal practices in the typical firm, new internal knowledge is weakly transformed from the knowledge of one individual to the knowledge of a firm. Instead, this new knowledge remains as know-how that belongs to one individual or a small community-of-practice.

Internal learning alone is not enough, external learning is needed to enhance the knowledge base. The high number and diversity of sources from which the High Performer obtains new knowledge foster its external learning process. In addition, its innovation management practices help assimilate and combine new external knowledge with existing knowledge. Instead, the typical firm has its strengths in internal learning. While the internal learning process increases shared knowledge among the staff members, it does not enlarge the knowledge base of the typical firm. Finally, the High Performer has balanced the external and internal learning processes. The internal learning process improves its knowledge and abilities by using the internal resources and experiences while the High Performer creates new knowledge and abilities through interaction with its external partners.

Thus, the gap between the High Performer and the typical firm is located in external learning process and to the degree of balance between the internal and external learning processes. Instead, the typical firm has the efficient internal learning process. The innovation engine proposes that the typical firm should take the first step by assessing whether in its partner network there exist unexploited opportunities to stimulate external learning. In addition, the typical small firm should assess the direction of sources from which they can obtain relevant new knowledge. Finally, the intensity of using these sources should be monitored.

Especially if the typical firm intends to change radically its directions, there is an urgent need to enlarge the current internal knowledge base through external learning to the new specific areas that are important for achieving the new goals. However, the typical firm has weak and informal activities to incorporate this external knowledge into its current knowledge. This is an issue that demands the development of formal procedures in the typical firm.

Finally, it should be noted that the internal and external learning processes complement each other. The internal learning process strengthens the firm's own knowledge base and the controllability of it while the external learning process is needed to enlarge this knowledge base. Thus, internal learning is a prerequisite for external learning. Therefore, these two processes should be in balance. Also this is an issue that should be assessed and reflected in the typical firm.

In summary, the innovation process together with the learning process are in the key roles to influence how efficiently a firm transforms its innovation potential into innovation performance. It is time to move on to explore how to identify whether the innovation efforts have resulted in the desired outcome.

7.7 Multidimensional Innovation Performance

As mentioned at the beginning of this chapter, the High Performers have been very successful in terms of business success. Please note that they HAVE BEEN very successful. It should be kept in mind that performance is an outcome of the past activities and it does not necessarily predict the degree of future success. For that reason, the innovation engine recommends that innovation performance should be considered from the four different aspects, all of them having the different time spans.

First, innovation output should be identified immediately after the completion of innovation activities. It demonstrates the direct results of the innovation process and its activities. As regards the innovation output of the High Performer, it has developed several innovation types including both the product and process innovations as well as the incremental and radical innovations. In addition, its innovation process produces these outputs on a regular basis. Instead, the typical firm has developed only occasionally an incremental product innovation. Thus, there is a risk that the way how this innovation is produced and delivered to customers is becoming inefficient and obsolete. In addition, it is evident that the low diversity of innovation activities limits the opportunities for learning in the typical firm.

Second, also the impact on customer should be measured. This can be done within the few months since a new offering is delivered to customers and they are using it. Based on its market-related success, the High Performer has high customer satisfaction. The typical firm has close relationships with customers and it is aware of how well its offerings fulfill their needs. However, regarding the customer deliveries, the typical firm must carry out continuous modifications for correcting prior errors or missing features. While these are done efficiently and without delays, in a longer term they affect customer satisfaction as well as efficiency-related performance. Hence, the typical firm should design a systematic procedure to monitor the customer impact. It is also needed to learn from mistakes.

Regarding the third aspect, business success, a longer time period is needed to measure it. The High Performer has sustained its long-term market-related and efficiency-related performance reflecting the abilities for creating high value for customers and maximizing value appropriation. Instead, while the typical firm has somewhat average efficiency-related performance, it is struggling with market-related performance. In order to sustain business success, the typical firm should try to achieve a balance between these two. However, it should be noted that business success is the result of past activities and the other elements of the innovation engine presented above are the drivers of it.

The fourth aspect, future potentiality, tries to capture effects that in a longer term may feed the performance drivers by enhancing the abilities of firms to respond to the external challenges and the unexpected actions of competitors. The High Performer with its sophisticated innovation management practices and the efficient learning processes are used to taking advantage from the past innovation efforts. Instead, the typical firm should start establishing these practices into its operations. This can be done by formalizing the practices that enable the feedback collection and reflection for the learning purposes.

7.8 Final Thoughts

This book offered a set of insights, views and frameworks to help meet the challenges of small firms to innovate, compete and grow. It has also presented a number of different kinds of pathways to superior or lost competitiveness. Yet, the fact remains that it is extremely difficult to create a winning recipe for success in small firms. However, it is clear that success is highly correlated with the abilities of these firms to learn and change. Based on the empirical evidence used in this book, small firms have quite high abilities to develop innovations. Instead, they should learn to compete and grow through these innovations.

Along with the journey we have assessed and even rated small firms in terms of their innovation activities, innovation capacity, growth and competitiveness and finally provided a system, the innovation engine, to be used for managing innovation in the context of small business. I hope that this has helped you get closer to successful innovation and profitable growth in small firms.

Now that we are at the end of the book, I urge you go on and assess the current state of your own firm. This may give you a sense of innovation and the performance of it across a variety of innovation facets. By assessing the extent and quality of your own innovation activities your may be able to identify the areas for improvements. On the other hand, you may recognize the unrealized potential in your firm. I wish you luck on your next journey.

Appendix

Details Behind the Figures

A.1 Empirical Evidence

The empirical evidence used in this book is based on two firm-level datasets. The first dataset consists of self-reported information on the innovation development of small firms, their capacity to innovate and the types of networking benefits gained for enhancing this capacity. This dataset also includes indicators to assess how satisfied the firms are with their business environment and how satisfied the employees are with the region as a place to work and live in. It also provides information on how the firms through collaboration have used the services provided by the regional business development agencies, universities and RD organizations, and other educational institutions.

This first dataset that has been extracted from the data collected at the beginning of 2009 for a larger research project exploring innovation in small firms covers four years from 2005 to 2008. Information is provided by the owner-managers of these firms.

The second dataset is a longitudinal panel data covering a period of 10 years (2003–2012). It consists of operationally defined longitudinal data on business performance, competitiveness and growth. It comprises the annual key figures of the financial statements covering the period of 10 years from 2003 to 2012.

Table A1.1.   Data used in this book.

Firm size by the no. of employees	Manufacturing		Service		Total	
	N	%	N	%	N	%
1–4	42	21.3	98	50.3	140	35.7
5–9	31	15.7	42	21.5	73	18.6
10–19	57	28.9	25	12.8	82	20.9
20–49	67	34.0	30	15.4	97	24.7
Total	197	100	195	100	392	100

This information has been drawn from the Trade Register Database provided by the National Board of Patents and Registration of Finland. The total number of cases included in the data is 392. Table A1.1 presents the data grouped by the sector and the size of a firm in terms of the number of employees.

The coding principles of manufacturing and service sectors follow the Standard Industrial Classification (SIC) and the division into sub-sectors has been made by adopting the classification introduced by Castaldi [2009].

A.2 Chapter 2 — Supportive Material

The Classification Analysis was used to observe whether the firms were on the basis of their innovation activities grouped into the innovation performer profiles as predicted. Based on it, the classification works quite well for each group. According to the results, 93.1% of the firms are correctly classified. Within the groups, 100.0% of the Low Performers, 100.0% of the Incremental Performers, 92.1% of the Radical Performers and 79.0% of the High Performers are classified as predicted.

Due to the fact that the number of employees reported by the firms includes both the full-time and part-time contracts, the calculatory number of full-time employees is used as a measure of firm size. The calculatory number of employees has been counted by dividing the annual paid salaries of a firm by the average annual salary paid to the private sector employee in the year in question. The basis for calculating the relative changes in the calculatory number of full-time employees is the period of 2003–2004.

Table A2.1.   Innovation patterns by the innovation performer profiles.

	Low Performer	Incremental Performer	Radical Performer	High Performer	Total
Manufacturing businesses					
N	32	90	29	46	197
Radical innovation activities[a]					
Product/service	—	—	75.9	67.4	26.9
Technical process	—	—	65.5	43.5	19.8
Administrative process	—	—	55.2	37.0	16.8
Incremental innovation activities[a]					
Product/service	25.0	88.9	20.7	95.7	70.1
Technical process	9.4	85.6	17.2	82.6	62.4
Administrative process	15.6	92.2	17.2	58.7	60.9
Diversity of innovation activities[b]	0.5	2.7	2.5	3.9	2.6
Service businesses					
N	29	73	34	59	195
Radical innovation activities[a]					
Product/service	—	—	88.2	84.7	41.0
Technical process	—	—	38.2	33.9	16.9
Administrative process	—	—	61.8	23.7	17.9
Incremental innovation activities[a]					
Product/service	31.0	93.2	32.4	76.3	68.2
Technical process	3.4	68.5	38.2	88.1	59.5
Administrative process	31.0	84.9	5.9	74.6	60.0
Diversity of innovation activities[b]	0.7	2.5	2.7	3.8	2.6

Notes: [a]Innovation activities refer to the proportion of firms that have developed the innovation type in question during the period of four years (2005–2008).

[b]Diversity refers to the number of different types of innovation activities during the period of four years (2005–2008).

A.3 Chapter 3 — Supportive Material

Table A3.1.   The items of innovation capability variables.

	Mean	Std	Cronbach's Alpha
Knowledge absorption			0.67
Capabilities to recognize relevant external knowledge	0.15	0.6	—
Capabilities to internalize new external knowledge	0.07	0.6	—
Capabilities to seize new opportunities for developing new solutions	0.13	0.6	—
Exploitation capabilities			0.68
Capabilities to exploit new knowledge for innovations	0.13	0.6	—
Capabilities to improve existing products and services	0.24	0.6	—
Capabilities to exploit innovations developed by others	−0.08	0.6	—
Capabilities to quickly implement change	0.09	0.7	—
Capabilities to increase sales to existing customers	0.08	0.6	—
Exploration capabilities			0.77
Capabilities to generate new innovations which differ from competitors' offerings	−0.05	0.7	—
Capabilities to expand to new markets	−0.15	0.7	—
Capabilities to acquire new customers	−0.05	0.6	—
Abilities to create new profitable business	−0.07	0.6	—
Risk management capabilities			0.70
Capabilities for risk assessment	−0.06	0.6	—
Willingness to risk taking	−0.13	0.7	—
Abilities for risk taking	−0.18	0.6	—

Note: Scale: −1 = not important, 0 = neutral, +1 = important.

Table A3.2.   Investments in RD by innovation performer profile.

	Low Performer %	Incremental Performer %	Radical Performer %	High Performer %	Total %
Manufacturing businesses					
<1%	59.4	45.6	24.1	6.5	35.5
1–2%	18.8	28.9	27.6	47.8	31.5
3–5%	3.1	15.6	17.2	17.4	14.2
>5%	—	3.3	17.2	26.1	10.2
Do not know	18.8	6.7	13.8	2.2	8.6
Total	100	100	100	100	100
Service businesses					
<1%	65.5	34.2	29.4	18.6	33.3
1–2%	10.3	27.4	20.6	20.3	21.5
3–5%	3.4	11.0	11.8	28.8	15.4
>5%	6.9	4.1	26.5	30.5	16.4
Do not know	13.8	23.3	11.8	1.7	13.3
Total	100	100	100	100	100

A.4 Chapter 4 — Supportive Material

Table A4.1.   Growth figures of the manufacturing businesses.

	Low Performer	Incremental Performer	Radical Performer	High Performer	Total
Absolute sales (€1,000,000)					
2003–2004	1.58	1.04	0.99	1.67	1.16
2005–2006	1.70	1.25	1.40	2.31	1.47
2007–2008	2.44	1.95	2.03	2.92	2.29
2009–2010	1.32	1.69	1.08	2.10	1.78
2011–2012	1.66	1.83	2.01	2.30	2.01
Absolute operating profits (€1,000)					
2003–2004	76.1	60.3	27.1	97.4	67.2
2005–2006	28.3	96.2	44.4	137.4	72.9
2007–2008	80.7	140.0	46.3	196.2	134.4
2009–2010	9.4	26.3	−0.9	64.9	16.0
2011–2012	34.2	58. 5	35.8	36.8	40.6
Absolute paid salaries (€1,000)					
2003–2004	400.5	338.6	447.5	400.5	386.7
2005–2006	494.8	411.4	532.6	542.8	476.1
2007–2008	528.7	547.1	779.5	690.4	575.2
2009–2010	439.6	479.8	594.6	748.8	538.9
2011–2012	452.3	523.6	715.9	792.6	610.0

Note: Median values (M) are used to minimize the effects of extreme values.

Table A4.2.   Growth figures of the service businesses.

	Low Performer	Incremental Performer	Radical Performer	High Performer	Total
Absolute sales (€1,000,000)					
2003–2004	0.37	0.38	0.49	0.37	0.38
2005–2006	0.43	0.54	0.55	0.38	0.48
2007–2008	0.45	0.59	0.65	0.77	0.62
2009–2010	0.46	0.59	0.69	0.72	0.64
2011–2012	0.41	0.62	0.69	0.63	0.61
Absolute operating profits (€1,000)					
2003–2004	33.7	27.9	27.1	18.6	27.1
2005–2006	32.8	31.1	22.3	31.7	30.8
2007–2008	52.1	36.3	31.5	50.7	45.2
2009–2010	29.0	25.7	12.2	36.9	27.3
2011–2012	31.2	15.2	30.7	23.6	23.3
Absolute paid salaries (€1,000)					
2003–2004	172.0	106.7	126.7	159.4	142.2
2005–2006	186.8	213.4	202.4	216.4	213.4
2007–2008	211.6	260.7	220.3	297.0	252.2
2009–2010	227.0	271.5	189.9	317.5	282.9
2011–2012	189.9	270.7	151.6	351.8	259.2

Note: Median values (M) are used to minimize the effects of extreme values.

Reference

Castaldi, C. (2009). The relative weight of manufacturing and services in Europe: An innovation perspective, *Technological Forecasting and Social Change*, 76(6), pp. 709–722.

Index

Printed in the United States
By Bookmasters